Math in Focus
Singapore Math®
by Marshall Cavendish

Workbook

Consultant and Author
Dr. Fong Ho Kheong

Authors
Gan Kee Soon and Chelvi Ramakrishnan

U.S. Consultants
Dr. Richard Bisk, Andy Clark, and Patsy F. Kanter

mc Marshall Cavendish
Education

U.S. Distributor

Houghton
Mifflin
Harcourt

COMMON
CORE

Published by Marshall Cavendish Education
Times Centre, 1 New Industrial Road, Singapore 536196
Customer Service Hotline: (65) 6213 9444
US Office Tel: (1-914) 332 8888 | Fax: (1-914) 332 8882
E-mail: tmesales@mceducation.com
Website: www.mceducation.com

Distributed by
Houghton Mifflin Harcourt
222 Berkeley Street
Boston, MA 02116
Tel: 617-351-5000
Website: www.hmheducation.com/mathinfocus

First published 2009
2013 Edition

Math in Focus® Grade 5 Workbook A
ISBN 978-0-669-01393-1

Printed in Singapore

16 17   1401   18
4500696050   A B C D E

Contents

1 Whole Numbers

2 Whole Number Multiplication and Division

3 Fractions and Mixed Numbers

4 Multiplying and Dividing Fractions and Mixed Numbers

5 Algebra

6 Area of a Triangle

7 Ratio

BLANK

Name: _____   Date: _____

1 Whole Numbers

Practice 1 Numbers to 10,000,000

Count on or back by *ten thousands* or *hundred thousands*. Then fill in the blanks.

1. 40,000 50,000 60,000 <u>70,000</u> <u>80,000</u>

2. 900,000 800,000 700,000 <u>600,000</u> <u>500,000</u>

Complete the table. Then write the number in standard form and in word form.

3.

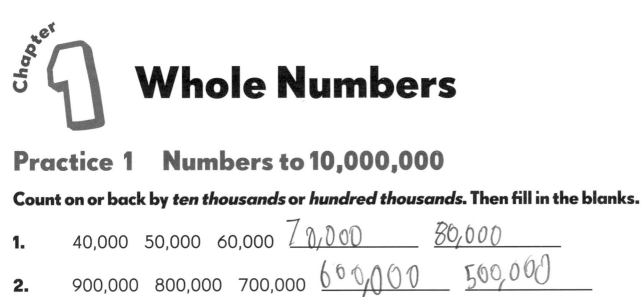

Hundred Thousands	Ten Thousands	Thousands	Hundreds	Tens	Ones
●● ●●	●●	●● ●●	●●●	●	●●● ●●●

	Standard Form	Word Form
4 hundred thousands	400,000	four hundred thousand
2 ten thousands	20,000	tweny thousand
5 thousands	5,000	five thousnd
3 hundreds	300	three hundred
1 ten	10	ten
6 ones	6	six

Number in standard form: <u>425,316</u>

Number in word form: <u>four hundred twenty five</u>
<u>thousand three hundred ten+six</u>

Write each number in standard form.

4.

Hundred Thousands	Ten Thousands	Thousands	Hundreds	Tens	Ones
●●	●●●	●●●●●●●●●	●●●●●●	●●●●●	●●●

The number is ___2 39,653___.

5.

Hundred Thousands	Ten Thousands	Thousands	Hundreds	Tens	Ones
●●●●●●●●	●●●	●●●●●	●●●●●●	●●	

The number is ___835,720___.

6. eight hundred sixteen thousand, nine hundred forty-three   ___816,943___

First, read the thousands period: eight hundred sixteen thousand — 816,000
Then, read the remaining period: nine hundred forty-three — 943

7. six hundred five thousand, five hundred   ___605,500___

8. one hundred three thousand, thirty-one   ___103,031___

9. eight hundred seventy thousand, three   ___870,003___

10. three hundred thousand, twelve   ___300,012___

Fill in the headings. Write *Tens*, *Hundreds*, *Ten Thousands*, or *Hundred Thousands*. Then write each number in word form.

11.

hundred thousands	ten thousands	Thousands	hundreds	tens	Ones
●		●●●●●	●●●	●●●●●●	●●

The number is _one hundred five thousand three hundred sixty-two_.

12.

hundred thousands	ten thousands	Thousands	hundreds	tens	Ones
●●●●●	●●●●●●			●●	●

The number is _five hundred sixty thousand twenty-one_.

Write each number in word form.

> 65,000 — sixty-five thousand
> 142 — one hundred forty-two

13. 65,142 _sixty-five thousand one hundred forty-two_

14. 368,400 _three hundred sixty eight thousand four hundred_

Complete to express each number in word form.

15.	802,101	eight hundred two thousand, one hundred _one_
16.	324,306	three hundred twenty-four _thousand_, three hundred six
17.	150,260	one hundred fifty thousand, _two_ hundred sixty
18.	999,198	nine hundred _ninety nine_ thousand, one hundred _ninety eight_

Use the table showing the populations of some cities to answer the questions.

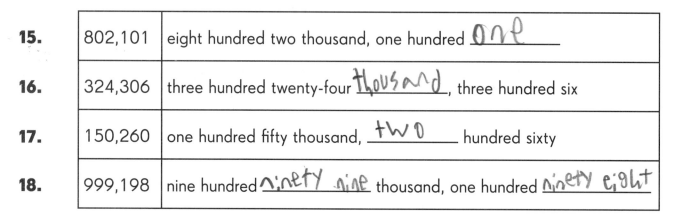

City	Population
Jacksonville, Florida	773,781
Hyde Park, New York	9,523
Portland, Oregon	538,544
Pittsburgh, Pennsylvania	312,819
Lexington, Massachusetts	30,355
Newport, Rhode Island	26,136

19. Write the population of Pittsburgh in word form.

three hundred twelve thousand eight hundred ninety nine

20. Which city has the least population? What is its population?

© Marshall Cavendish International (Singapore) Private Limited.

Practice 2   Numbers to 10,000,000

Complete the table. Then write the number in standard form and in word form.

1.

Millions	Hundred Thousands	Ten Thousands	Thousands	Hundreds	Tens	Ones
⬤⬤ ⬤⬤ ⬤⬤ ⬤⬤ ⬤⬤	⬤	⬤ ⬤⬤ ⬤⬤	⬤⬤ ⬤⬤ ⬤⬤	⬤ ⬤⬤	⬤⬤ ⬤⬤	⬤⬤

	Standard Form	Word Form
☐ millions		
☐ hundred thousand		
☐ ten thousands		
☐ thousands		
☐ hundreds		
☐ tens		
☐ ones		

Number in standard form: _____

Number in word form: _____

_____

Write the number in standard form and in word form.

2.

Millions	Hundred Thousands	Ten Thousands	Thousands	Hundreds	Tens	Ones
⦿⦿⦿	⦿⦿	⦿⦿⦿⦿				

Number in standard form: _____

Number in word form: _____

Write each number in standard form.

3. two million, one hundred fifty-six thousand, four   _____

4. five million, two hundred thirty-eight thousand   _____

5. seven million, one hundred fifty thousand   _____

6. six million, sixty thousand, fifty   _____

7. three million, three   _____

Write each number in word form.

8. 5,050,000 _____

9. 8,147,600 _____

_____

10. 7,230,014 _____

_____

11. 5,192,622 _____

_____

12. 9,009,009 _____

Practice 3   Place Value

Complete. Use the place-value chart.

Hundred Thousands	Ten Thousands	Thousands	Hundreds	Tens	Ones
○○○	○○ ○○	○○ ○○○	○○		○
3	4	5	2	0	1

In 345,201:

1. a. the digit 3 stands for _____.   **b.** the value of the digit 3 is _____.

2. a. the digit 4 stands for _____.   **b.** the value of the digit 4 is _____.

3. a. the digit 5 stands for _____.   **b.** the value of the digit 5 is _____.

Write the value of each digit in the correct box.

4.

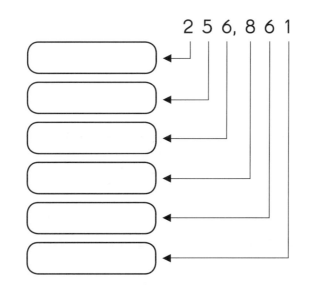

2 5 6, 8 6 1

Complete.

In 346,812:

5. the digit 3 stands for _____.

6. the digit 6 stands for _____.

Write the value of the digit 2 in each number.

7. 3**2**9,051 _____   **8.** 903,5**2**1 _____

9. 71**2**,635 _____   **10.** **2**58,169 _____

Complete.

11. In 320,187, the digit _____ is in the thousands place.

12. In 835,129, the digit 8 is in the _____ place.

13. In 348,792, the digit 4 is in the _____ place.

Complete to express each number in expanded form.

14. 153,420 = 100,000 + _____ + 3,000 + 400 + 20

15. 760,300 = _____ + 60,000 + 300

16. 700,000 + 8,000 + 500 + 4 = _____

17. 200,000 + 2,000 + 10 = _____

Complete. Use the place-value chart.

Millions	Hundred Thousands	Ten Thousands	Thousands	Hundreds	Tens	Ones
1	5	0	8	3	6	9

In 1,508,369:

18. **a.** the digit 1 stands for _____.

  b. the value of the digit 1 is _____.

19. **a.** the digit 8 stands for _____.

  b. the value of the digit 8 is _____.

20. the digit 0 is in the _____ place.

Write the value of each digit in the correct box.

21.

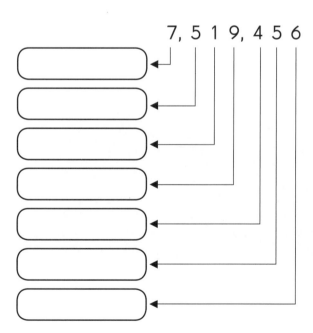

7, 5 1 9, 4 5 6

Complete.

22. In 5,420,000, the digit 5 is in the _____ place.

23. In 1,077,215, the digit in the hundred thousands place is _____.

24. In 9,400,210, the digit 9 stands for _____.

Complete to express each number in expanded form.

25. 4,130,000 = _____ + 100,000 + 30,000

26. 6,123,750 = 6,000,000 + 100,000 + 20,000 + 3,000 + 700 + _____

27. 7,550,100 = 7,000,000 + _____ + 50,000 + 100

28. 5,000,000 + 200,000 + 7,000 + 70 = _____

29. 3,000,000 + 20,000 + 9,000 + 100 + 5 = _____

Read the clues to find the number.

> It is a 7-digit number.
> The value of the digit 7 is 700.
> The greatest digit is in the millions place.
> The digit 1 is next to the digit in the millions place.
> The value of the digit 8 is 8 tens.
> The value of the digit 3 is 3 ones.
> The digit 5 is in the thousands place.
> The digit 6 stands for 60,000.

30. The number is _____.

© Marshall Cavendish International (Singapore) Private Limited.

Practice 4   Comparing Numbers to 10,000,000

Complete the place-value chart. Then use it to compare the numbers.

1.   Which is greater, 197,210 or 225,302?

> Compare the values of the digits, working from left to right.

Hundred Thousands	Ten Thousands	Thousands	Hundreds	Tens	Ones

_____ hundred thousands is greater than _____ hundred thousand.

So, _____ is greater than _____.

Fill each ◯ with > or <.

2.   128,758 ◯ 74,906   **3.**   523,719 ◯ 523,689

4.   89,000 ◯ 712,758   **5.**   635,002 ◯ 635,100

Circle the least number and cross out the greatest number.

6.   375,061   172,503   127,203   157,203   371,560   371,605

Order the numbers from least to greatest.

7.   739,615   795,316   315,679   615,379

_____

8.   245,385   805,342   97,632   300,596

_____

Compare the numbers. Use the place-value chart to help you.

9.

Millions	Hundred Thousands	Ten Thousands	Thousands	Hundreds	Tens	Ones
8	0	7	9	7	2	0
6	9	9	0	3	9	5

_____ millions is less than _____ millions.

_____ is less than _____.

10.

Millions	Hundred Thousands	Ten Thousands	Thousands	Hundreds	Tens	Ones
1	0	8	3	9	5	2
5	0	9	6	3	5	7

_____ is greater than _____.

11.

Millions	Hundred Thousands	Ten Thousands	Thousands	Hundreds	Tens	Ones
6	4	1	2	5	8	6
6	4	3	8	6	7	1

_____ is greater than _____.

Fill each ◯ with > or <.

12. 4,015,280 ◯ 2,845,000

13. 999,098 ◯ 1,000,000

14. 2,007,625 ◯ 2,107,625

15. 7,405,319 ◯ 905,407

Order the numbers from greatest to least.

16. 2,432,000   480,000   2,720,000   3,190,000

_____

17. 513,900   3,150,000   913,000   2,020,000

_____

Find the missing numbers.

18. 738,561   938,561   1,138,561   ...

   a. 938,561 is _____ more than 738,561.

   b. 1,138,561 is _____ more than 938,561.

   c. _____ more than 1,138,561 is _____.

   d. The next number in the pattern is _____.

19. 4,655,230   4,555,230   4,455,230   ...

   a. 4,555,230 is _____ less than 4,655,230.

   b. 4,455,230 is _____ less than 4,555,230.

   c. _____ less than 4,455,230 is _____.

   d. The next number in the pattern is _____.

Find the rule. Then complete the number patterns.

20. 230,180   231,180   232,180   _____   _____

Rule: _____

21. 850,400   845,400   840,400   _____   _____

Rule: _____

22. 2,650,719   3,650,719   4,650,719   _____   _____

Rule: _____

23. 6,298,436   5,198,436   4,098,436   _____   _____

Rule: _____

Complete.

24. 5,083,000 = 5,000,000 + _____ + 3,000   Ⓜ

25. 5,000,000 + 600,000 + 2,000 = _____   Ⓣ

26. Which is greater, 509,900 or 562,000? _____   Ⓢ

27. Which is less, 1,020,000 or 1,002,000? _____   Ⓐ

28. The value of the digit 1 in 7,120,000 is _____.   Ⓟ

What goes around the world but remains in one corner?
Write the letters that match the answers below to find out.

_____   _____   _____   _____   _____

562,000   5,602,000   1,002,000   80,000   100,000

Practice 5   Rounding and Estimating

**Mark an X to show where each decimal is located on the number line.
Then round each number.**

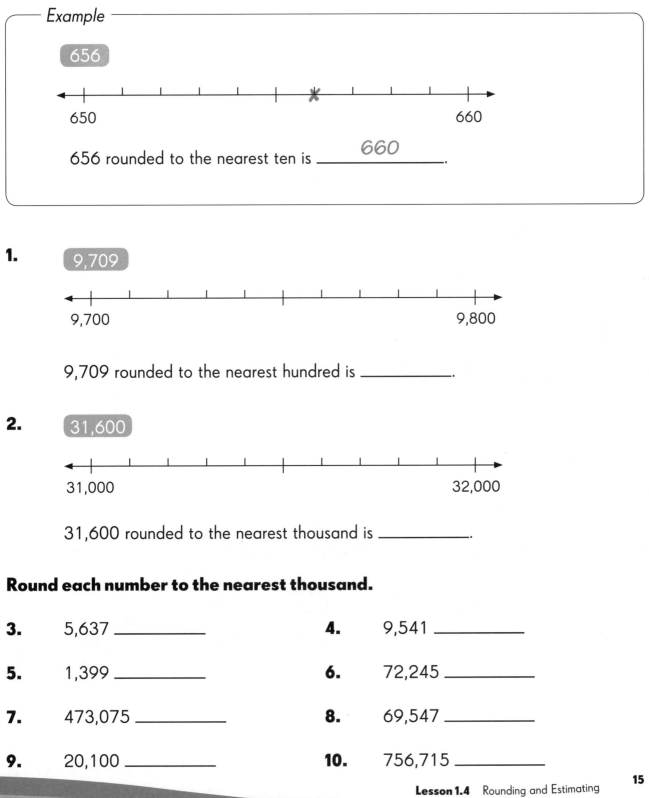

Example

656

650   660

656 rounded to the nearest ten is _____660_____.

1.   9,709

9,700   9,800

9,709 rounded to the nearest hundred is _____.

2.   31,600

31,000   32,000

31,600 rounded to the nearest thousand is _____.

Round each number to the nearest thousand.

3.   5,637 _____   **4.**   9,541 _____

5.   1,399 _____   **6.**   72,245 _____

7.   473,075 _____   **8.**   69,547 _____

9.   20,100 _____   **10.**   756,715 _____

Answer each question. Use the number line to help you.

Rounding to the nearest thousand, what is the least and the greatest number that rounds to 3,000?

Least
2,500

3,000

Greatest
3,499

2,000   2,500   3,000   4,000

3,400   3,500

Least number: _____2,500_____

Greatest number: _____3,499_____

11. Rounding to the nearest thousand, what is

a. the least number that rounds to 5,000?

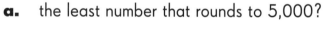

4,000   4,500   5,000   5,500   6,000

_____

b. the greatest number that rounds to 90,000?

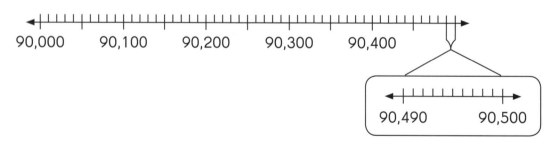

90,000   90,100   90,200   90,300   90,400

90,490   90,500

_____

Round each number to the nearest thousand. Then estimate the sum.

> **Example**
>
> 9,286 + 5,703
>
> *9,286 rounds to 9,000.*
> *5,703 rounds to 6,000.*
> *9,000 + 6,000 = 15,000*

12.   6,789 + 4,200

13.   7,264 + 7,153

14.   4,885 + 6,075

15.   3,105 + 9,940

16.   7,083 + 2,607

Round each number to the nearest thousand. Then estimate the difference.

Example

8,156 − 6,109

8,156 rounds to 8,000.
6,109 rounds to 6,000.
8,000 − 6,000 = 2,000

17. 4,924 − 4,127

18. 7,105 − 3,940

19. 4,885 − 1,075

20. 3,522 − 2,815

21. 6,480 − 1,397

Use front-end estimation with adjustment to estimate each sum.

Example

1,963 + 3,290 + 7,837

1,000 + 3,000 + 7,000
= 11,000

900 + 200 + 800
= 1,900

To the nearest thousand:
1,900 → 2,000

11,000 + 2,000 = 13,000

22.   2,541 + 6,061 + 1,681

23.   7,823 + 6,848 + 3,310

24.   4,197 + 8,936 + 2,226

Use front-end estimation with adjustment to estimate each difference.

25. $6,770 - 3,081$

> *Example*
>
> $2,943 - 1,272$
>
> $2,000 - 1,000$
> $= 1,000$
>
> $900 - 200 = 700$
>
> To the nearest thousand:
> $700 \rightarrow 1,000$
>
> $1,000 + 1,000 = 2,000$

26. $8,764 - 3,589$ **27.** $7,802 - 4,396$

Use front-end estimation with adjustment to estimate each difference.

Example

7,594 − 2,831

7,000 − 2,000 = 5,000

800 − 500 = 300

To the nearest thousand:
300 → 0

5,000 − 0 = 5,000

28.   5,780 − 3,962

29.   9,119 − 4,852

30.   8,254 − 4,836

Estimate each product.

> **Example**
>
> 4,512 × 2
>
> 4,512 rounds to 5,000.
> 5,000 × 2 = 10,000

31. 3,765 × 7

32. 2,521 × 5

33. 5,108 × 6

34. 8,497 × 9

35. 6,060 × 3

Estimate each quotient.

> **Example**
>
> 2,786 ÷ 5
>
> 2,786 rounds to 3,000.
> 3,000 ÷ 5 = 600

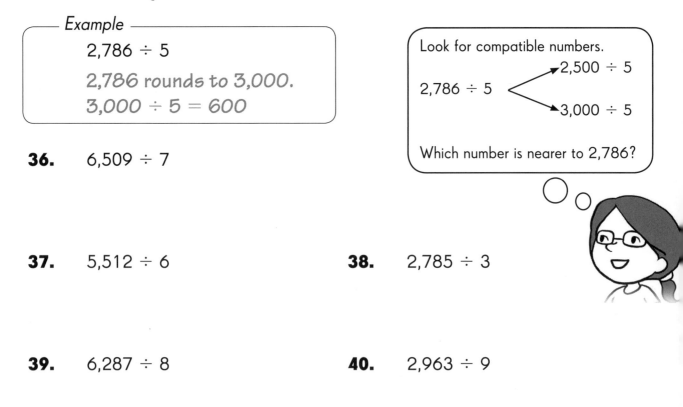

Look for compatible numbers.

2,786 ÷ 5

2,500 ÷ 5

3,000 ÷ 5

Which number is nearer to 2,786?

36. 6,509 ÷ 7

37. 5,512 ÷ 6

38. 2,785 ÷ 3

39. 6,287 ÷ 8

40. 2,963 ÷ 9

Math Journal

1. Kim and Dominic found the sum of 8,642 and 9,328.

| Kim's answer is 17,970. | Dominic's answer is 1,890. |

One of their answers is incorrect.
Show how you could use estimation to check which answer is reasonable.

2. Samantha found these quotients.

  a. 7,986 ÷ 8 = 998 R 2   **b.** 2,659 ÷ 3 = 264 R 3

Show how you could check whether the quotients are reasonable.
State in each case whether the quotient is reasonable.

3. Lisa was asked to round

  a. 763 to the nearest hundred.

  b. 3,730 to the nearest thousand.

Lisa rounded 763 to 700 and 3,730 to 3,000. What mistakes did she make?
What should the correct answer in each case have been?

Put On Your Thinking Cap!

Challenging Practice

Arrange the digits to form three 6-digit numbers that will round to 756,000 when rounded to the nearest thousand.

Put On Your Thinking Cap!

Problem Solving

1. What number can you subtract from 3,200 such that their difference is
a 4-digit number that has:
the digit 2 in the thousands place,
the digit 3 in the hundreds place and
zeros in the tens and ones place?

2. A 3-digit number when divided by 5 has an even quotient. When it is
divided by 3, it also has an even quotient.

   a. What is the digit in the ones place?

   b. What can the number be?

Whole Number Multiplication and Division

Chapter 2

Practice 1   Using a Calculator

Add.

1.   215 + 9,843 = _____

2.   6,789 + 18 = _____

3.   97 + 8,154 = _____

4.   1,693 + 8,157 = _____

Subtract.

5.   8,215 − 79 = _____

6.   6,286 − 129 = _____

7.   2,159 − 1,998 = _____

8.   26,145 − 9,354 = _____

Multiply.

9.   359 × 12 = _____

10.   217 × 58 = _____

11.   1,975 × 5 = _____

12.   7,050 × 8 = _____

Divide.

13.   504 ÷ 9 = _____

14.   4,104 ÷ 6 = _____

15.   8,160 ÷ 85 = _____

16.   17,604 ÷ 18 = _____

Only one path after each problem has the correct answer.
Trace Flavio's path by choosing the paths with the correct answers.

17.

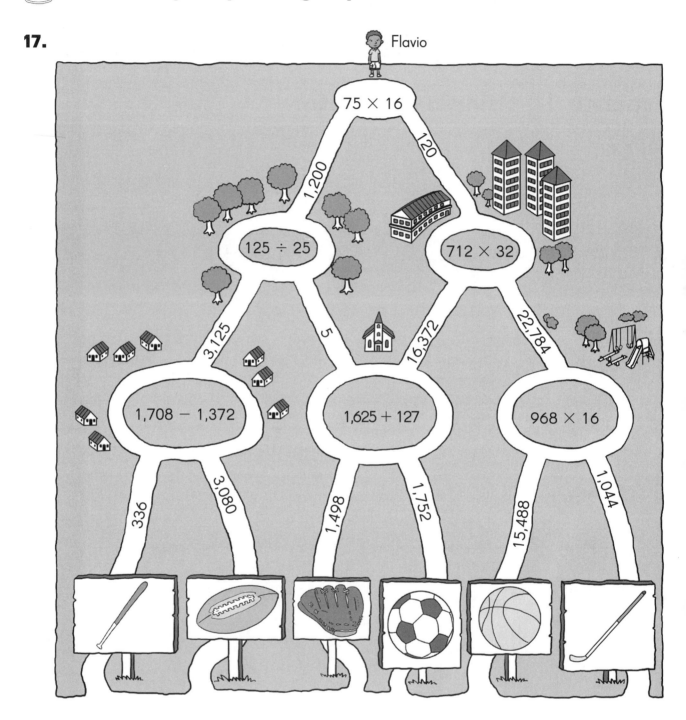

The prize at the end of Flavio's path is:

_____

Practice 2   Multiplying by Tens, Hundreds, or Thousands

Multiply.

1.   47 × 10 = _____

2.   38 × 10 = _____

3.   109 × 10 = _____

4.   521 × 10 = _____

5.   7,140 × 10 = _____

6.   1,503 × 10 = _____

7.   3,702 × 10 = _____

8.   9,342 × 10 = _____

Find the missing factors.

9.   96 × _____ = 960

10.   _____ × 10 = 700

11.   514 × _____ = 5,140

12.   _____ × 10 = 5,000

13.   308 × _____ = 3,080

14.   _____ × 10 = 4,020

15.   2,096 × _____ = 20,960

16.   _____ × 10 = 91,760

Complete.

17. 39×30

$= (39 \times \underline{\quad\quad}) \times 10$

$= \underline{\quad\quad} \times 10$

$= \underline{\quad\quad}$

18. 143×90

$= (143 \times \underline{\quad\quad}) \times \underline{\quad\quad}$

$= \underline{\quad\quad} \times \underline{\quad\quad}$

$= \underline{\quad\quad}$

19. 360×30

$= (360 \times \underline{\quad\quad}) \times \underline{\quad\quad}$

$= \underline{\quad\quad} \times \underline{\quad\quad}$

$= \underline{\quad\quad}$

20. 285×80

$= (285 \times \underline{\quad\quad}) \times \underline{\quad\quad}$

$= \underline{\quad\quad} \times \underline{\quad\quad}$

$= \underline{\quad\quad}$

Multiply.

21.   7 × 1,000 = _____   Ⓡ

22.   86 × 100 = _____   Ⓣ

23.   70 × 1,000 = _____   Ⓐ

24.   95 × 100 = _____   Ⓔ

25.   400 × 1,000 = _____   Ⓛ

26.   217 × 100 = _____   Ⓟ

27.   726 × 1,000 = _____   Ⓘ

28.   803 × 100 = _____   Ⓢ

29.   8,032 × 1,000 = _____   Ⓞ

30.   3,810 × 100 = _____   Ⓑ

31.   3,936 × 1,000 = _____   Ⓝ

What cat has long, fine hair, and a snubbed nose?
Write the letters that match the answers below to find out.

| 21,700 | 9,500 | 7,000 | 80,300 | 726,000 | 70,000 | 3,936,000 |

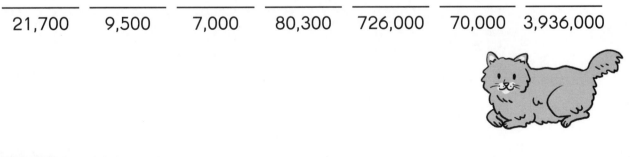

Find the missing factors.

32. $17 \times$ _____ $= 1,700$

33. _____ $\times 1,000 = 25,000$

34. _____ $\times 1,000 = 478,000$

35. $320 \times$ _____ $= 320,000$

36. $1,315 \times$ _____ $= 131,500$

37. _____ $\times 1,000 = 2,662,000$

38. $4,668 \times$ _____ $= 466,800$

39. _____ $\times 100 = 576,000$

Complete.

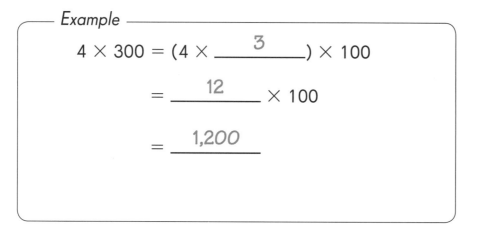

Example

$$4 \times 300 = (4 \times \underline{\quad 3 \quad}) \times 100$$

$$= \underline{\quad 12 \quad} \times 100$$

$$= \underline{\quad 1,200 \quad}$$

40. $12 \times 500 = (12 \times$ _____ $) \times 100$

$$= \underline{\quad\quad} \times 100$$

$$= \underline{\quad\quad}$$

41. $700 \times 900 = (700 \times$ _____ $) \times 100$

$$= \underline{\quad\quad} \times 100$$

$$= \underline{\quad\quad}$$

Name: _____ **Date:** _____

Complete.

42. 814×700

$= (814 \times \underline{\hspace{1.5cm}}) \times 100$

$= \underline{\hspace{1.5cm}} \times 100$

$= \underline{\hspace{1.5cm}}$

43. $5,400 \times 800$

$= (5,400 \times \underline{\hspace{1.5cm}}) \times 100$

$= \underline{\hspace{1.5cm}} \times 100$

$= \underline{\hspace{1.5cm}}$

44. $5 \times 7,000$

$= (5 \times \underline{\hspace{1.5cm}}) \times 1,000$

$= \underline{\hspace{1.5cm}} \times 1,000$

$= \underline{\hspace{1.5cm}}$

45. $8 \times 5,000$

$= (8 \times \underline{\hspace{1.5cm}}) \times 1,000$

$= \underline{\hspace{1.5cm}} \times 1,000$

$= \underline{\hspace{1.5cm}}$

46. $12 \times 3,000$

$= (12 \times \underline{\hspace{1.5cm}}) \times 1,000$

$= \underline{\hspace{1.5cm}} \times 1,000$

$= \underline{\hspace{1.5cm}}$

47. $15 \times 2,000$

$= (15 \times \underline{\hspace{1.5cm}}) \times 1,000$

$= \underline{\hspace{1.5cm}} \times 1,000$

$= \underline{\hspace{1.5cm}}$

48. $300 \times 4,000$

$= (300 \times \underline{\hspace{1.5cm}}) \times 1,000$

$= \underline{\hspace{1.5cm}} \times 1,000$

$= \underline{\hspace{1.5cm}}$

49. $663 \times 6,000$

$= (663 \times \underline{\hspace{1.5cm}}) \times 1,000$

$= \underline{\hspace{1.5cm}} \times 1,000$

$= \underline{\hspace{1.5cm}}$

Multiply.

	Multiplying by Tens	Multiplying by Hundreds	Multiplying by Thousands
50.	17×70 =	17×700 =	$17 \times 7,000$ =
51.	65×30 =	65×300 =	$65 \times 3,000$ =
52.	90×40 =	90×400 =	$90 \times 4,000$ =
53.	812×10 =	812×100 =	$812 \times 1,000$ =
54.	634×20 =	634×200 =	$634 \times 2,000$ =

Find the missing factors.

55. $31 \times$ _____ $= 3,100$

56. $30 \times$ _____ $= 90,000$

57. $103 \times$ _____ $= 3,090$

58. $25 \times$ _____ $= 5,000$

The owner of an electronics store wants to estimate the amount she will receive from the sales of these items:

> 58 all-in-one printers at $219 each.
> 652 radio clocks at $73 each.
> 99 portable audio players at $217 each.
> 39 plasma television sets at $4,156 each.

Estimate the amount she receives for each type of item by rounding to the greatest place value. Then, estimate the total amount from the sales of the items.

59.   58 × $219 rounds to _____ × $_____ = $ _____

60.   652 × $73 rounds to _____ × $ _____ = $ _____

61.   99 × $217 rounds to _____ × $ _____ = $ _____

62.   39 × $4,156 rounds to _____ × $ _____ = $ _____

63.   The total estimated amount is

$ _____ + $ _____ + $ _____ + $ _____

= $ _____

Math Journal

Multiply. Explain how you can check if your answer is reasonable.

184×97

Practice 3   Multiplying by 2-Digit Numbers

Multiply. Estimate to check if your answers are reasonable.

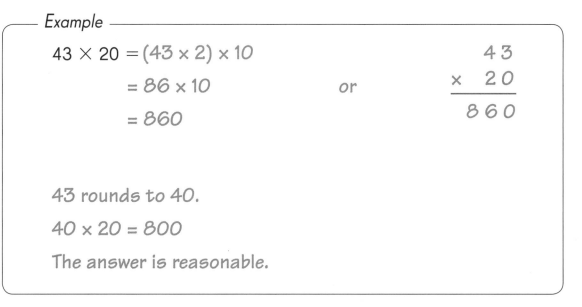

Example

$$43 \times 20 = (43 \times 2) \times 10$$
$$= 86 \times 10$$
$$= 860$$

or

```
    4 3
  × 2 0
  ─────
  8 6 0
```

43 rounds to 40.

$40 \times 20 = 800$

The answer is reasonable.

1. $59 \times 40 =$

2. $91 \times 14 =$

3. $96 \times 15 =$

4. $23 \times 17 =$

Multiply. Estimate to check if your answers are reasonable.

Example

$510 \times 30 = (510 \times 3) \times 10$

$= 1{,}530 \times 10$ or

$= 15{,}300$

$$\begin{array}{r} 5\ 1\ 0 \\ \times\ \ \ 3\ 0 \\ \hline 1\ 5,\ 3\ 0\ 0 \end{array}$$

510 rounds to 500.

$500 \times 30 = 15{,}000$

The answer is reasonable.

5. $750 \times 60 =$ **6.** $614 \times 31 =$

7. $556 \times 47 =$ **8.** $843 \times 25 =$

Multiply. Estimate to check if your answers are reasonable.

Example

$1{,}970 \times 20 = (1{,}970 \times 2) \times 10$

$\phantom{1{,}970 \times 20} = 3{,}940 \times 10$

$\phantom{1{,}970 \times 20} = 39{,}400$

or

$$\begin{array}{r} 1{,}9\,7\,0 \\ \times \qquad 2\,0 \\ \hline 3\,9{,}4\,0\,0 \end{array}$$

1,970 rounds to 2,000.

$2{,}000 \times 20 = 40{,}000$

The answer is reasonable.

9. $3{,}610 \times 60 =$

10. $8{,}142 \times 16 =$

11. $5{,}193 \times 35 =$

12. $4{,}563 \times 29 =$

Multiply. Estimate to check if your answers are reasonable.

13. $85 \times 35 =$

14. $78 \times 21 =$

15. $738 \times 96 =$

16. $921 \times 57 =$

17. $3,072 \times 82 =$

18. $7,846 \times 63 =$

Math Journal

Jodi estimated these products.

a. 2,892 × 21 rounds to 3,000 × 20 = 60,000

b. 2,743 × 18 rounds to 3,000 × 20 = 60,000

She then worked out the actual answers. Even though the estimated answers were the same, Jodi found that the actual answers were very different from each other.

1. In which case is the estimate closer to the actual answer?
Explain why.

2. If an estimate does not make your answer seem reasonable, what can you do to make sure you have done your work correctly?

Practice 4   Dividing by Tens, Hundreds, or Thousands

Complete.

1.   100 ÷ 10 = _____

2.   670 ÷ 10 = _____

3.   1,050 ÷ _____ = 105

4.   _____ ÷ 10 = 1,974

5.   52,260 ÷ 10 = _____

6.   30,500 ÷ _____ = 3,050

Complete.

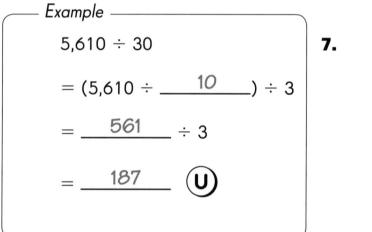

Example

5,610 ÷ 30

= (5,610 ÷ __10__) ÷ 3

= __561__ ÷ 3

= __187__ (U)

7.   3,000 ÷ 60

= (3,000 ÷ 10) ÷ _____

= _____ ÷ 6

= _____ (M)

8.   1,040 ÷ 40

= (1,040 ÷ _____) ÷ _____

= _____ ÷ _____

= _____ (A)

Complete.

9.   8,700 ÷ 60

= (8,700 ÷ _____) ÷ _____

= _____ ÷ _____

= _____ (T)

10.   3,450 ÷ 50

= (3,450 ÷ _____) ÷ _____

= _____ ÷ _____

= _____ (R)

11.   34,230 ÷ 70

= (34,230 ÷ _____) ÷ _____

= _____ ÷ _____

= _____ (N)

Which U.S. president had a sign on his desk that said 'The buck stops here'?
Write the letters on pages 43 and 44 that match the answers below to find out.

HARRY S. _____ _____ _____ _____ _____ _____
                 145   69   187   50   26   489

Divide.

12.   3,400 ÷ 100 = _____   (P)

13.   560,000 ÷ 1,000 = _____   (H)

14.   5,000 ÷ 100 = _____   (S)

15.   38,000 ÷ 1,000 = _____   (I)

16.   7,700 ÷ 100 = _____   (N)

17.   360,000 ÷ 1,000 = _____   (M)

18.   2,000 ÷ 100 = _____   (B)

19.   415,000 ÷ 1,000 = _____   (A)

To which class of animals does the salamander belong?
Write the letters that match the answers below to find out.

____	____	____	____	____	____	____	____	____	____
415	360	34	560	38	20	38	415	77	50

Complete.

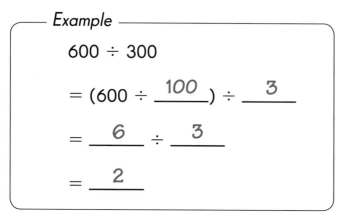

20. $1,600 \div 400$

    $= (1,600 \div \underline{\hspace{1cm}}) \div \underline{\hspace{1cm}}$

    $= \underline{\hspace{1cm}} \div \underline{\hspace{1cm}}$

    $= \underline{\hspace{1cm}}$

21. $81,000 \div 900$

    $= (81,000 \div \underline{\hspace{1cm}}) \div \underline{\hspace{1cm}}$

    $= \underline{\hspace{1cm}} \div \underline{\hspace{1cm}}$

    $= \underline{\hspace{1cm}}$

22. $31,500 \div 500$

    $= (31,500 \div \underline{\hspace{1cm}}) \div \underline{\hspace{1cm}}$

    $= \underline{\hspace{1cm}} \div \underline{\hspace{1cm}}$

    $= \underline{\hspace{1cm}}$

Complete.

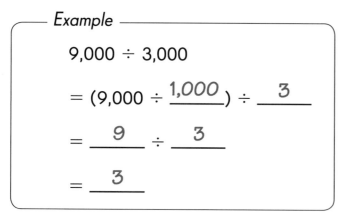

23. $56,000 \div 7,000$

    $= (56,000 \div \underline{\hspace{1cm}}) \div \underline{\hspace{1cm}}$

    $= \underline{\hspace{1cm}} \div \underline{\hspace{1cm}}$

    $= \underline{\hspace{1cm}}$

24. $133,000 \div 7,000$

    $= (133,000 \div \underline{\hspace{1cm}}) \div \underline{\hspace{1cm}}$

    $= \underline{\hspace{1cm}} \div \underline{\hspace{1cm}}$

    $= \underline{\hspace{1cm}}$

25. $120,000 \div 8,000$

    $= (120,000 \div \underline{\hspace{1cm}}) \div \underline{\hspace{1cm}}$

    $= \underline{\hspace{1cm}} \div \underline{\hspace{1cm}}$

    $= \underline{\hspace{1cm}}$

Divide.

	Dividing by Tens	Dividing by Hundreds	Dividing by Thousands
26.	360 ÷ 40 =	3,600 ÷ 400 =	36,000 ÷ 4,000 =
27.	1,190 ÷ 70 =	11,900 ÷ 700 =	119,000 ÷ 7,000 =
28.	12,680 ÷ 20 =	126,800 ÷ 200 =	1,268,000 ÷ 2,000 =
29.	23,200 ÷ 80 =	232,000 ÷ 800 =	2,320,000 ÷ 8,000 =

Complete.

30.   430 ÷ _____ = 43

31.   9,000 ÷ _____ = 30

32.   49,000 ÷ _____ = 7

33.   2,400 ÷ _____ = 120

34.   64,000 ÷ _____ = 160

35.   85,000 ÷ _____ = 17

Estimate each quotient.

Example

$6{,}452 \div 27$ rounds to ___*6,000*___ $\div$ ___*30*___ = ___*200*___

36. $7{,}865 \div 41$ rounds to _____ $\div$ _____ = _____

37. $9{,}125 \div 345$ rounds to _____ $\div$ _____ = _____

38. $9{,}825 \div 206$ rounds to _____ $\div$ _____ = _____

39. $7{,}226 \div 871$ rounds to _____ $\div$ _____ = _____

40. $5{,}299 \div 49$ rounds to _____ $\div$ _____ = _____

41. $3{,}654 \div 27$ rounds to _____ $\div$ _____ = _____

What number can be evenly divided by 3, 7, and 9?
Color the numbers below that match the answers above to find out.

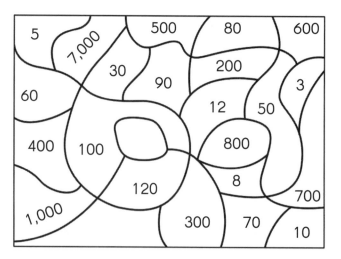

Practice 5   Dividing by 2-Digit Numbers

Divide.

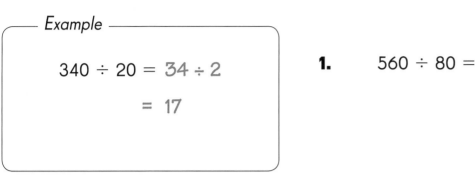

Example

$$340 \div 20 = 34 \div 2$$
$$= 17$$

1. $560 \div 80 =$

2. $630 \div 60 =$

3. $590 \div 30 =$

4. $190 \div 90 =$

5. $360 \div 50 =$

Divide.

Example

$43 \div 12$

12 rounds to 10.
$4 \times 10 = 40$
The quotient is about 4.
$4 \times 12 = 48$
The estimated quotient is too big. Try 3.

$$\begin{array}{r} 3 \text{ R } 7 \\ 12\overline{)4\ 3} \\ 3\ 6 \\ \hline 7 \end{array}$$

$43 \div 12 = 3 \text{ R } 7$

6. $98 \div 16 =$

7. $65 \div 24 =$

8. $94 \div 37 =$

Divide.

┌─ *Example* ──────────────────────┐

$215 \div 51$

215 rounds to 200.

$4 \times 50 = 200$

The quotient is about 4.

```
        4 R 11
51) 2 1 5
    2 0 4
    ─────
      1 1
```

$215 \div 51 = 4 \text{ R } 11$

└──────────────────────────────────┘

9. $362 \div 60 =$

10. $178 \div 45 =$

11. $850 \div 88 =$

12. $273 \div 59 =$

Divide.

Example

$354 \div 14$

$$
\begin{array}{r}
2\ 5\ \text{R}\ 4 \\
14\overline{)3\ 5\ 4} \\
2\ 8 \\
\hline
7\ 4 \\
7\ 0 \\
\hline
4
\end{array}
$$

3 hundreds 5 tens = 35 tens

35 tens $\div$ 14 = 2 tens R 7 tens

7 tens 4 ones = 74 ones

$74 \div 14 = 5$ R 4

$354 \div 14 = 25$ R 4

---

13. $850 \div 17 =$

14. $546 \div 25 =$

15. $700 \div 28 =$

16. $936 \div 43 =$

Divide.

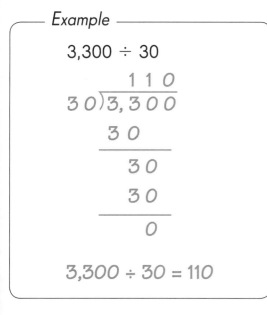

Example

$$3{,}300 \div 30$$

$$\begin{array}{r} 1\ 1\ 0 \\ 30 \overline{)3{,}300} \\ 3\ 0 \\ \hline 30 \\ 30 \\ \hline 0 \end{array}$$

$$3{,}300 \div 30 = 110$$

17. $7{,}500 \div 60 =$

18. $9{,}607 \div 15 =$

19. $5{,}007 \div 18 =$

20. $3{,}215 \div 22 =$

21. $8{,}012 \div 46 =$

Play tic-tac-toe using the exercises below .

9	7	6
2	0	3
5	1	4

Choose 5 problems below and circle them. Work out the problems you chose. Find those remainders in the grid. Cross them out.
Did you win the game?

22.   27 ÷ 12

23.   58 ÷ 19

24.   457 ÷ 28

25.   406 ÷ 25

26.   518 ÷ 43

27.   642 ÷ 58

28.   6,900 ÷ 75

29.   1,286 ÷ 21

30.   2,995 ÷ 83

Practice 6   Order of Operations

Simplify. Record each step.

Example

$18 - 11 - 4 =$ _____3_____

Step 1 ____18 – 11 = 7____

Step 2 ____7 – 4 = 3____

1. $26 + 8 - 19 =$ _____

Step 1 _____

Step 2 _____

2. $12 + 16 - 9 + 3 =$ _____

Step 1 _____

Step 2 _____

Step 3 _____

3. $58 - 23 + 11 - 6 =$ _____

Step 1 _____

Step 2 _____

Step 3 _____

Simplify. State the order in which you performed the operations.

Numeric Expression	Order of Operations Performed		
	First	**Second**	**Third**
$12 + 14 + 9 = 35$	+	+	
4. $60 + 18 - 7$			
5. $70 - 15 - 49$			
6. $23 + 16 - 7 + 12$			
7. $15 - 12 + 17 - 6$			

Simplify. Record each step.

Example

$9 \times 6 \div 2 =$ _____27_____

Step 1 _____$9 \times 6 = 54$_____

Step 2 _____$54 \div 2 = 27$_____

8. $25 \times 3 \div 5 =$ _____

Step 1 _____

Step 2 _____

9. $200 \div 10 \times 3 \div 5 =$ _____

Step 1 _____

Step 2 _____

Step 3 _____

10. $250 \div 5 \div 10 \times 2 =$ _____

Step 1 _____

Step 2 _____

Step 3 _____

Simplify. State the order in which you performed the operations.

Numeric Expression	Order of Operations Performed		
	First	**Second**	**Third**
$30 \times 2 \times 5 = 300$	$\times$	$\times$	
11. $6 \times 10 \div 5$			
12. $28 \div 7 \times 4$			
13. $40 \div 8 \div 5$			
14. $20 \div 10 \times 8 \div 2$			
15. $120 \div 12 \div 2 \times 16$			

Simplify. Record each step.

┌─ Example ─────────────────────────┐
│   │
│ $7 \times 8 - 6 = $ ___50___   │
│   │
│   **Step 1** ___$7 \times 8 = 56$___ │
│   │
│   **Step 2** ___$56 - 6 = 50$___ │
│   │
└───────────────────────────────────┘

16. $14 + 9 \times 7 = $ _____

Step 1 _____

Step 2 _____

17. $200 \div 20 + 5 = $ _____

Step 1 _____

Step 2 _____

18. $80 - 16 \div 4 = $ _____

Step 1 _____

Step 2 _____

Simplify. State the order in which you performed the operations.

Numeric Expression	Order of Operations Performed	
	First	**Second**
$25 - 5 \times 3 = 10$	$\times$	$-$
19. $90 + 16 \div 8$		
20. $83 - 72 \div 6$		
21. $5 + 90 \times 7$		
22. $240 \div 20 + 15$		
23. $7 \times 80 - 160$		

Simplify. Record each step.

— *Example* —

$54 \div 6 + 20 \times 4 = \underline{\quad 89 \quad}$

Step 1 $\underline{\quad 54 \div 6 = 9 \quad}$

Step 2 $\underline{\quad 20 \times 4 = 80 \quad}$

Step 3 $\underline{\quad 9 + 80 = 89 \quad}$

24. $40 - 6 + 10 \times 3 = \underline{\qquad}$

Step 1 $\underline{\qquad\qquad}$

Step 2 $\underline{\qquad\qquad}$

Step 3 $\underline{\qquad\qquad}$

25. $36 \div 6 - 25 \div 5 = \underline{\qquad}$

Step 1 $\underline{\qquad\qquad}$

Step 2 $\underline{\qquad\qquad}$

Step 3 $\underline{\qquad\qquad}$

26. $25 \times 4 - 36 \div 9 = \underline{\qquad}$

Step 1 $\underline{\qquad\qquad}$

Step 2 $\underline{\qquad\qquad}$

Step 3 $\underline{\qquad\qquad}$

Simplify. State the order in which you performed the operations.

Numeric Expression	Order of Operations Performed			
	First	Second	Third	Fourth
$60 \div 3 + 14 \times 2 = 48$	÷	×	+	
27. $20 - 5 \times 2 + 6$				
28. $13 - 6 \times 2 + 12 \div 4$				
29. $27 \div 3 + 40 \times 6$				
30. $64 - 60 + 12 \times 3$				
31. $42 \div 7 - 2 + 7$				

Simplify. Record each step.

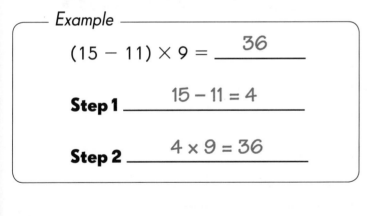

Example

$(15 - 11) \times 9 = \underline{\hspace{1em} 36 \hspace{1em}}$

Step 1 $\underline{\hspace{1em} 15 - 11 = 4 \hspace{1em}}$

Step 2 $\underline{\hspace{1em} 4 \times 9 = 36 \hspace{1em}}$

32. $(11 + 5) \div 16 = \underline{\hspace{2em}}$

Step 1 _____

Step 2 _____

Simplify. Record each step.

33. $63 - (9 \times 7) =$ _____

       Step 1 _____

       Step 2 _____

34. $32 \div (14 + 2) =$ _____

       Step 1 _____

       Step 2 _____

Simplify. State the order in which you performed the operations.

	Numeric Expression	Order of Operations Performed	
		First	**Second**
	$3 \times (72 \div 8) = 27$	$(\div)$	$\times$
35.	$(40 \div 5) \times 11$		
36.	$(36 - 15) \times 2$		
37.	$36 - (15 \times 2)$		
38.	$(62 + 10) \div 6$		
39.	$70 \div (16 - 9)$		

Simplify. Record each step.

Example

$21 + (12 + 6) \div 3 =$ ___27___

Step 1 ___12 + 6 = 18___

Step 2 ___18 \div 3 = 6___

Step 3 ___21 + 6 = 27___

40. $7 + (8 - 4) \times 10 =$ _____

Step 1 _____

Step 2 _____

Step 3 _____

41. $32 \div (7 + 1) \times 9 - 5 =$ _____

Step 1 _____

Step 2 _____

Step 3 _____

Step 4 _____

Simplify. Record each step.

42. $(47 + 12) - 10 \div 5 \times 3 =$ _____

Step 1 _____

Step 2 _____

Step 3 _____

Step 4 _____

Simplify. State the order in which you performed the operations.

Numeric Expression	Order of Operations Performed			
	First	Second	Third	Fourth
$100 + (720 + 200) \div 2$ $= 560$	(+)	$\div$	+	
43. $24 \times 5 - (125 - 80)$				
44. $360 \div (98 + 22) \times 19 - 30$				
45. $11 + (34 + 16) \div 5$				
46. $7 \times 6 - (18 - 6)$				
47. $21 \div (2 + 5) \times 12 - 8$				

Practice 7 Real-World Problems: Multiplication and Division

Solve. Show your work.

1. Rafael has 118 baseball cards arranged in an album. Each page of the album can hold 9 cards. How many pages are full and how many cards are on the last page?

2. A ski club had 146 members. Each member paid $30 a month for training fees. How much did the club collect in fees for the year?

Solve. Show your work.

3.   A farmer collects 1,250 eggs on a morning. She puts 30 eggs on each tray. How many egg trays does she need to hold all the eggs?

4.   At a supermarket, pineapple juice sells at $1 per pint (16 ounces). Greg wants to buy eighteen 40-ounce cans of pineapple juice from the supermarket. How much does he have to pay altogether?

Name: _____   Date: _____

Solve. Show your work.

5. [calculator icon] A charitable organization spends $4,500 giving out food vouchers to families.

    a. Each family receives one voucher worth $25. How many families are there?

    b. Each voucher will be worth $32 next year. How much more money will the charity need next year?

6. A group of tourists visits an art museum. The admission is $13 for each adult and $7 for each child. There are 10 adults and 18 children in the group. How much do they pay altogether?

Solve. Show your work.

7.   The length of a rectangular board is 10 centimeters longer than its width. The width of the board is 26 centimeters. The board is cut into 9 equal pieces.

   a.   What is the area of each piece?

   b.   What are the possible dimensions of each piece? (Take the dimensions to be whole numbers.)

8.   There are 912 yellow chairs and blue chairs altogether in an auditorium. The blue chairs are arranged in 36 rows with 12 chairs in each row. The yellow chairs are arranged in rows of 20. How many rows of yellow chairs are there?

Solve. Show your work.

9. The table shows the wages of workers in Siva's company. Siva works from Tuesday through Sunday each week. How much does he earn in 1 week?

Weekdays	$186 per day
Saturday and Sunday	$248 per day

Solve. Show your work.

10. The table shows the charges at a parking garage.

First hour	$8
Every additional $\frac{1}{2}$ hour	$3

a. Sharona parked her car at the garage from 9:30 A.M. to 11 A.M. on the same day. How much did she have to pay?

b. Daryll parked his car there from 9 A.M. to 12:30 P.M. on the same day. How much did he have to pay?

Practice 8   Real-World Problems: Multiplication and Division

Solve. Use any strategy.

1. Hannah and Francine have $120. Hannah and Peter have $230. Peter has 6 times as much money as Francine. How much money does Hannah have?

2. Larry is 10 years old and his sister is 7 years old. In how many years' time will their total age be 25 years?

Solve. Use any strategy.

3. A box of chalk and 2 staplers cost $10. Three boxes of chalk and 2 staplers cost $18. Find the total cost of 1 box of chalk and 1 stapler.

Solve. Use any strategy.

4.   Sally and Marta had the same number of postcards. After Sally sold
18 of her postcards, Marta had 4 times as many postcards as Sally.
How many postcards did each girl have to begin with?

Solve. Use any strategy.

5.   A basket with 12 apples has a mass of 3,105 grams. The same basket with 7 apples has a mass of 1,980 grams. Each apple has the same mass. What is the mass of the basket?

Math Journal

1.   Kelly has a 370-page sketch book. She wants to allocate an equal
number of pages for making sketches to each month of the year.
She uses division to find the number of pages she can possibly allocate
to each month, and the number of pages she will have left over.
She works out the division like this:

```
        3 0
   12 ) 3 7 0
        3 6 0
          1 0
```

Which part of the answer tells the number of pages that Kelly can
possibly allocate to each month?
Which part tells the number of pages left over?

2. Mark was asked to simplify the numeric expression 6 + 4 × 2. He worked out the steps like this:

$$6 + 4 \times 2 = 10 \times 2$$
$$= 20$$

Is he correct? Explain why.

3. Look at the following problem and the solution given by a student: Abel, Belle, and Cindy have $408 altogether. Belle has $7 more than Cindy and $5 more than Abel. How much does Abel have?

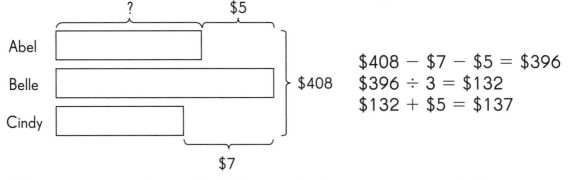

$408 − $7 − $5 = $396
$396 ÷ 3 = $132
$132 + $5 = $137

What was the mistake made? What should the correct answer be?

Put On Your Thinking Cap!

Challenging Practice

Solve. Use any strategy.

1. A sticker costs 15¢, and a packet of 8 similar stickers costs $1. Clement buys 37 stickers. What is the least amount of money that Clement spends on the stickers?

2. Forty members of a parents' organization are making candles to raise money. One member drops out and the rest have to make 3 more candles each to make up. Each member makes the same number of candles. How many candles do they make altogether?

Solve. Use any strategy.

3. Mr. Thomas puts up fence posts from one end of a field to the other, equal distances apart. There are 27 posts. The width of each post is 10 centimeters. The distance between two posts is 30 meters. Find the length of the fence.

4. Kirsten has 64 coins in her piggy bank. She has $9.25 in dimes and quarters. How many dimes and how many quarters does she have?

Put On Your Thinking Cap!

Problem Solving

Solve. Use any strategy.

1. Darcy, Jason, and Maria share $268. Jason has $20 more than Darcy
    and Maria has twice as much money as Jason. How much money do
    Darcy and Jason have altogether?

2. Juan and Rachel have the same number of marbles. Rachel gives
    away 10 marbles and Juan gives away 22 marbles. Rachel then has
    3 times as many marbles as Juan. How many marbles did each of
    them have at first?

Solve. Use any strategy.

3.   Gerry had a total of 30 pens and pencils. He decided to trade with his friends all his pens for pencils. If he traded every pen for 2 pencils, he would have 48 pencils in all. How many pens and how many pencils did he have before the trade?

Cumulative Review

for Chapters 1 and 2

Concepts and Skills

Write each number in standard form. *(Lesson 1.1)*

1. One hundred thousand, seventy _____

2. Five hundred sixty thousand _____

3. Five million, eighty thousand, five _____

4. Two million, four hundred thousand, seven hundred twenty _____

Write each number in word form. *(Lesson 1.1)*

5. 120,450 _____

_____

6. 500,312 _____

_____

7. 1,050,400 _____

_____

8. 5,732,800 _____

_____

Complete. *(Lesson 1.2)*

In 1,238,906:

9.   the digit 8 stands for _____.

10.   the digit 9 stands for _____.

11.   the digit 1 stands for _____.

State the value of the digit 3 in each number. *(Lesson 1.2)*

12.   538,426: _____

13.   1,**3**25,407: _____

Complete. *(Lesson 1.2)*

14.   In 807,456, the digit _____ is in the thousands place.

15.   In 5,486,302, the digit _____ is in the millions place.

16.   In 305,128, the digit 0 is in the _____ place.

17.   In 7,614,892, the digit 6 is in the _____ place.

18.   918,230 = _____ + 10,000 + 8,000 + 200 + 30

19.   538,417 = 500,000 + _____ + 8,000 + 400 + 10 + 7

20.   6,000,000 + 30,000 + 90 = _____

Fill each ( ) **with > or <.** *(Lesson 1.3)*

21.   185,263 ( ) 183,256   **22.**   5,060,345 ( ) 995,863

23.   899,506 ( ) 900,650   **24.**   231,623 ( ) 231,621

Order the number from greatest to least. *(Lesson 1.3)*

25.   528,010   1,280,500   258,100   528,100

_____

Find the rule. Then complete the number pattern. *(Lesson 1.3)*

26.   276,300   286,300   296,300   _____   _____

   Rule: _____

Estimate by rounding. *(Lesson 1.4)*

27.   7,512 + 3,281   _____

28.   6,528 − 5,938   _____

29.   1,592 × 5   _____

30.   2,576 ÷ 3   _____

Estimate using front-end estimation with adjustment. *(Lesson 1.4)*

31.   4,087 + 3,910 + 9,125

Estimate using front-end estimation with adjustment. *(Lesson 1.4)*

32. $8,685 + 6,319 + 7,752$

33. $5,879 - 1,143$

34. $7,974 - 2,660$

Complete. Remember to write the correct units in your answers. You may use your calculator where necessary. *(Lesson 2.1)*

35.   Find the area of a square that has sides of length 96 inches.

_____

36.   Ms. Suarez has $5,651. Mr. Knox. has $853 more than Ms. Suarez. How much does Mr. Knox have?

_____

Complete. Remember to write the correct units in your answers.
You may use your calculator where necessary. *(Lesson 2.1)*

37. There are 176 gallons of gas in Tank A. There are 19 gallons less gas in Tank B. How many gallons of gas are there in Tank B?

_____

38. A truck is loaded with 25 similar crates. The total weight of the crates is 2,000 pounds. What is the weight of each crate?

_____

Multiply. *(Lesson 2.2)*

39. $315 \times 10 =$ _____   **40.** $25 \times 100 =$ _____

41. $238 \times 1,000 =$ _____ **42.** $147 \times 50 =$ _____

43. $63 \times 200 =$ _____   **44.** $906 \times 7,000 =$ _____

Estimate by rounding. *(Lesson 2.2)*

45.   41 × 58 = _____

46.   297 × 32 = _____

47.   1,087 × 21 = _____

48.   4,975 × 78 = _____

Multiply. Estimate to check if your answers are reasonable. *(Lesson 2.3)*

49.   82 × 45 = _____   **50.**   78 × 21 = _____

51.   275 × 59 = _____   **52.**   738 × 96 = _____

Multiply. Estimate to check if your answers are reasonable. *(Lesson 2.3)*

53. 4,672 × 73 = _____

54. 8,781 × 26 = _____

Divide. *(Lesson 2.4)*

55. 3,560 ÷ 10 = _____

56. 1,900 ÷ 100 = _____

57. 17,000 ÷ 1,000 = _____

58. 900 ÷ 60 = _____

59. 96,000 ÷ 400 = _____

60. 504,000 ÷ 9,000 = _____

Estimate. *(Lesson 2.4)*

61. 4,593 ÷ 53 _____

62. 6,298 ÷ 164 _____

63. 7,623 ÷ 4,451 _____

64. 4,239 ÷ 73 _____

Divide. *(Lesson 2.5)*

65. 96 ÷ 16 = _____   **66.** 57 ÷ 23 = _____

67. 459 ÷ 27 = _____   **68.** 503 ÷ 15 = _____

Divide. *(Lesson 2.5)*

69. $9,229 \div 17 =$ _____   **70.** $4,749 \div 46 =$ _____

Simplify. *(Lesson 2.6)*

71. $60 + 12 - 36 =$ _____   **72.** $10 \times 9 \div 3 =$ _____

73. $29 + 42 \div 6 =$ _____   **74.** $(90 - 85) \times 7 =$ _____

75. $50 \times 8 + 12 \div 4 =$ _____   **76.** $69 \div 3 - 3 + 10 =$ _____

Problem Solving

Solve. Show your work.

77. Tony had an equal number of cranberry bars and walnut bars. He gave away 66 cranberry bars. He then had 4 times as many walnut bars as cranberry bars left. How many bars did he have at first?

78. Mrs. Turner had 20 yards of fabric at first. She made 5 similar curtains. She used 3 yards of fabric for making each curtain. Then she used another 2 yards of fabric to make a cushion cover. How much fabric does she have left?

Solve. Show your work.

79. At a school fair, a fifth-grade class sold 25 liters of orange juice.
The orange juice was sold in cups containing 200 milliliters and 300 milliliters.
An equal number of cups containing 200 milliliters and 300 milliliters were sold.
How many cups of orange juice did the class sell?

80. Mikhail used 220 inches of wire to make this figure.

The figure is made up of two identical triangles, a 15-inch by 12-inch
rectangle and a square of side 19 inches. What is the length of one
side of each triangle if all the sides of the triangles are equal in length?

Solve. Show your work.

81. A shop owner bought 260 handbags at 5 for $25. She then sold all of them at 2 for $18. How much money did she make?

82. Alan scored a total of 14 points for answering all the 15 questions on a math quiz. For every correctly answered question, Alan got 2 points. For every wrong answer, he lost 2 points. How many questions did he answer correctly?

Solve. Show your work.

83. Beth and Lewis buy the same amount of fish pellets. If Beth feeds her goldfish 14 fish pellets each day, a container of pellets will last 20 days. If Lewis feeds his goldfish 8 fish pellets each day, how many more days will the container of pellets last Lewis' goldfish?

84. Joan can pick 9 pounds of strawberries in one hour.

    a. How long does she take to pick 72 pounds of strawberries?

    b. Joan is paid $12 per hour. How much does Joan earn if she picks twice the total weight of strawberries in **a.**?

Solve. Show your work.

85. There are 2,488 students in Washington School. There are 160 more students in Kent School. The number of students in Bellow School is half the total number of students in Washington School and Kent School. How many students are there in Bellow School?

86. Jasmine mixes 1,250 milliliters of syrup with twice as much water to make lemonade. She then pours the lemonade equally into 15 glasses. How much lemonade does each glass contain? Give your answer in milliliters.

Chapter 3 Fractions and Mixed Numbers

Practice 1   Adding Unlike Fractions

Find two equivalent fractions for each fraction.

> *Example*
>
> $\dfrac{2}{3} = \dfrac{4}{6} \rule{2cm}{0.4pt} = \dfrac{6}{9} \rule{2cm}{0.4pt}$

1. $\dfrac{3}{4} = \rule{2cm}{0.4pt} = \rule{2cm}{0.4pt}$

2. $\dfrac{2}{5} = \rule{2cm}{0.4pt} = \rule{2cm}{0.4pt}$

3. $\dfrac{5}{6} = \rule{2cm}{0.4pt} = \rule{2cm}{0.4pt}$

4. $\dfrac{1}{7} = \rule{2cm}{0.4pt} = \rule{2cm}{0.4pt}$

Express each fraction in simplest form.

5. $\dfrac{6}{8} = \rule{2cm}{0.4pt}$

6. $\dfrac{8}{20} = \rule{2cm}{0.4pt}$

7. $\dfrac{10}{15} = \rule{2cm}{0.4pt}$

8. $\dfrac{9}{21} = \rule{2cm}{0.4pt}$

Rewrite each pair of unlike fractions as like fractions.

┌─ *Example* ─────────────────────────────┐

$\dfrac{1}{2}$ = $\dfrac{2}{4}$ $\dfrac{1}{4}$ = $\dfrac{1}{4}$

└──┘

9. $\dfrac{1}{4}$ = _____ $\dfrac{5}{12}$ = _____

10. $\dfrac{1}{10}$ = _____ $\dfrac{2}{5}$ = _____

11. $\dfrac{5}{9}$ = _____ $\dfrac{2}{3}$ = _____

12. $\dfrac{3}{8}$ = _____ $\dfrac{9}{16}$ = _____

Write equivalent fractions for each fraction. Then find the least common denominator of the fractions.

┌─ *Example* ─────────────────────────────┐

$\dfrac{1}{2}$ = $\dfrac{2}{4}$ = $\dfrac{3}{6}$

$\dfrac{2}{3}$ = $\dfrac{4}{6}$

The least common denominator

is ___6___.

└──┘

13. $\dfrac{2}{3}$ =

$\dfrac{3}{4}$ =

The least common denominator

is _____.

14. $\dfrac{1}{4}$ =

$\dfrac{5}{6}$ =

The least common denominator

is _____.

15. $\dfrac{5}{6}$ =

$\dfrac{3}{8}$ =

The least common denominator

is _____.

Shade and label each model to show the fractions. Then complete the addition sentence.

— *Example* —

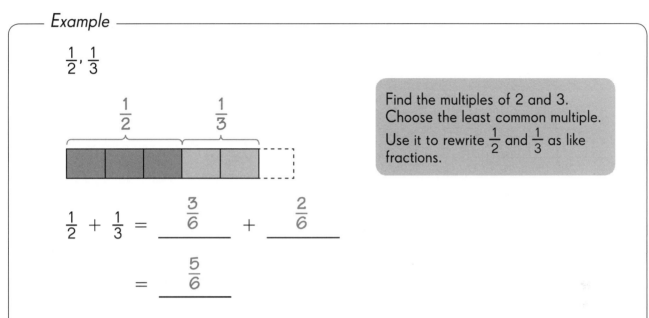

$\frac{1}{2}, \frac{1}{3}$

$\frac{1}{2}$ $\frac{1}{3}$

Find the multiples of 2 and 3. Choose the least common multiple. Use it to rewrite $\frac{1}{2}$ and $\frac{1}{3}$ as like fractions.

$\frac{1}{2} + \frac{1}{3} = \dfrac{\frac{3}{6}}{\rule{2cm}{0.4pt}} + \dfrac{\frac{2}{6}}{\rule{2cm}{0.4pt}}$

$= \dfrac{\frac{5}{6}}{\rule{2cm}{0.4pt}}$

16. $\frac{1}{5}, \frac{1}{2}$

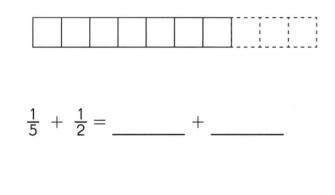

$\frac{1}{5} + \frac{1}{2} = \underline{\hspace{2cm}} + \underline{\hspace{2cm}}$

$= \underline{\hspace{2cm}}$

Shade and label each model to show the fractions. Then complete the addition sentence.

17. $\frac{1}{6}, \frac{1}{4}$

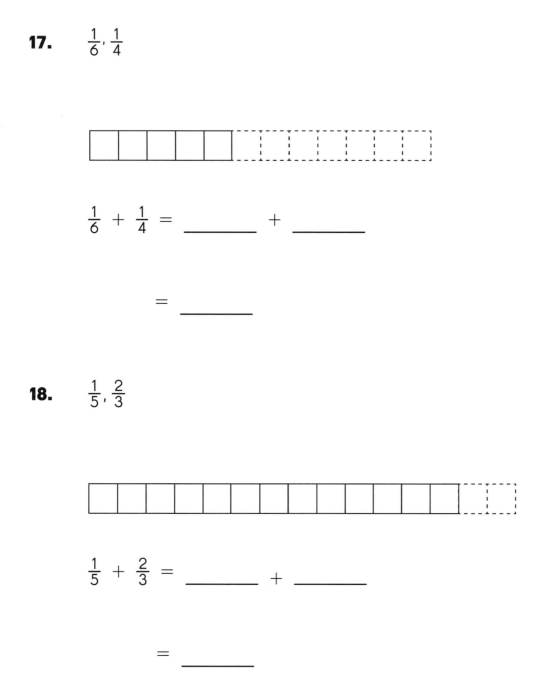

$\frac{1}{6} + \frac{1}{4} = $ _____ $+$ _____

$= $ _____

18. $\frac{1}{5}, \frac{2}{3}$

$\frac{1}{5} + \frac{2}{3} = $ _____ $+$ _____

$= $ _____

Look at the model. Write two addition sentences.

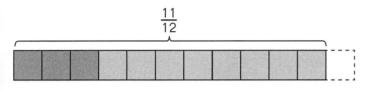

$\frac{11}{12}$

19. Addition sentence 1:

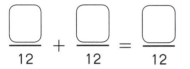

$$\frac{\boxed{}}{12} + \frac{\boxed{}}{12} = \frac{\boxed{}}{12}$$

20. Addition sentence 2 (fractions in simplest form):

_____ + _____ = _____

Add. Express each sum in simplest form.

21. $\frac{1}{3} + \frac{1}{9} =$

22. $\frac{5}{8} + \frac{2}{4} =$

23. $\frac{1}{2} + \frac{6}{7} =$

24. $\frac{4}{8} + \frac{1}{5} =$

Use benchmarks to estimate each sum.

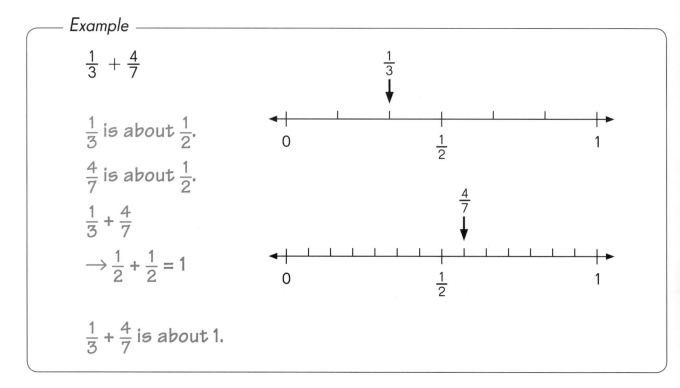

Example

$\frac{1}{3} + \frac{4}{7}$

$\frac{1}{3}$ is about $\frac{1}{2}$.

$\frac{4}{7}$ is about $\frac{1}{2}$.

$\frac{1}{3} + \frac{4}{7}$

$\rightarrow \frac{1}{2} + \frac{1}{2} = 1$

$\frac{1}{3} + \frac{4}{7}$ is about 1.

25. $\frac{2}{3} + \frac{2}{9}$

26. $\frac{7}{9} + \frac{1}{7} + \frac{3}{5}$

Practice 2   Subtracting Unlike Fractions

Rewrite the fractions as like fractions and complete the subtraction sentence.

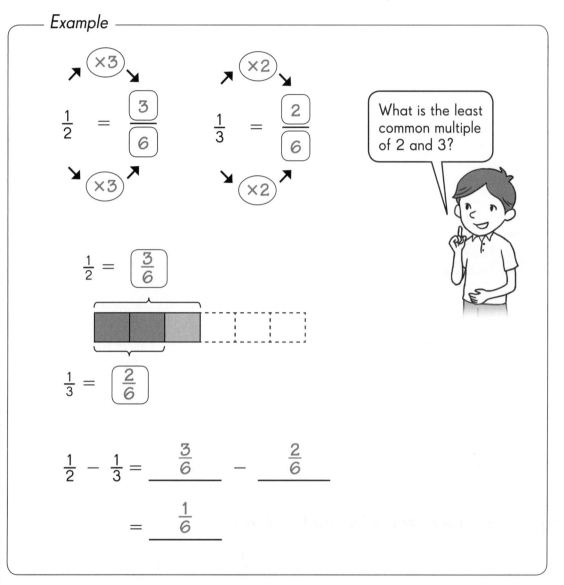

Example

$$\frac{1}{2} = \boxed{\frac{3}{6}}$$

$$\frac{1}{3} = \boxed{\frac{2}{6}}$$

What is the least common multiple of 2 and 3?

$$\frac{1}{2} = \boxed{\frac{3}{6}}$$

$$\frac{1}{3} = \boxed{\frac{2}{6}}$$

$$\frac{1}{2} - \frac{1}{3} = \underline{\quad \frac{3}{6} \quad} - \underline{\quad \frac{2}{6} \quad}$$

$$= \underline{\quad \frac{1}{6} \quad}$$

Rewrite the fractions as like fractions and complete the subtraction sentence.

1.

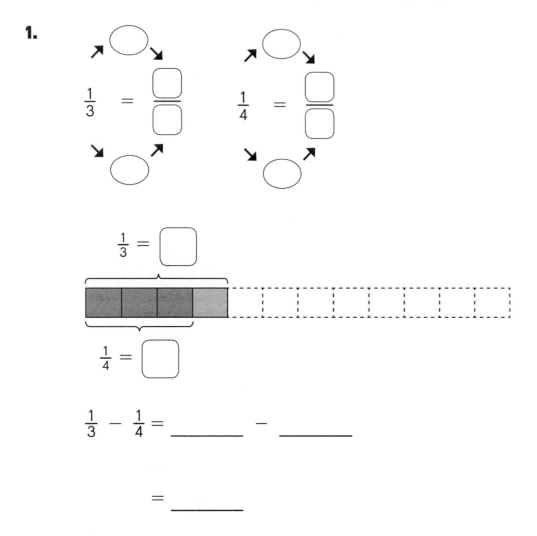

$$\frac{1}{3} = \frac{\Box}{\Box}$$

$$\frac{1}{4} = \frac{\Box}{\Box}$$

$$\frac{1}{3} = \Box$$

$$\frac{1}{4} = \Box$$

$$\frac{1}{3} - \frac{1}{4} = \underline{\hspace{1.5cm}} - \underline{\hspace{1.5cm}}$$

$$= \underline{\hspace{1.5cm}}$$

Subtract. Express each difference in simplest form.

2. $\dfrac{7}{12} - \dfrac{2}{4} =$

3. $\dfrac{4}{5} - \dfrac{1}{3} =$

4. $1 - \dfrac{5}{6} - \dfrac{1}{12} =$

5. $\dfrac{7}{9} - \dfrac{1}{6} =$

Use benchmarks to estimate each difference.

Example

$$\frac{4}{5} - \frac{3}{8}$$

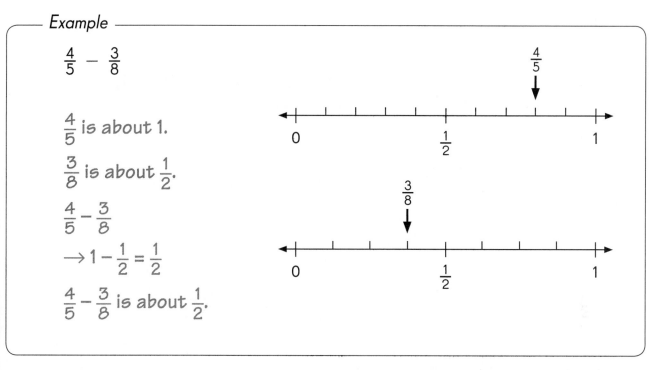

$\frac{4}{5}$ is about 1.

$\frac{3}{8}$ is about $\frac{1}{2}$.

$\frac{4}{5} - \frac{3}{8}$

$\rightarrow 1 - \frac{1}{2} = \frac{1}{2}$

$\frac{4}{5} - \frac{3}{8}$ is about $\frac{1}{2}$.

6. $\frac{9}{10} - \frac{1}{6}$

7. $\frac{5}{12} - \frac{1}{9}$

Math Journal

Darren drew a model to find $\frac{4}{5} - \frac{1}{2}$. His model is drawn incorrectly. Explain his mistakes. Then draw the correct model and find the difference.

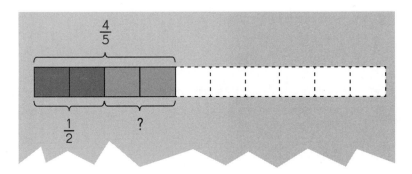

Darren's model is wrong because:

The correct model is:

Practice 3 Fractions, Mixed Numbers, and Division Expressions

Look at the diagram. Complete.

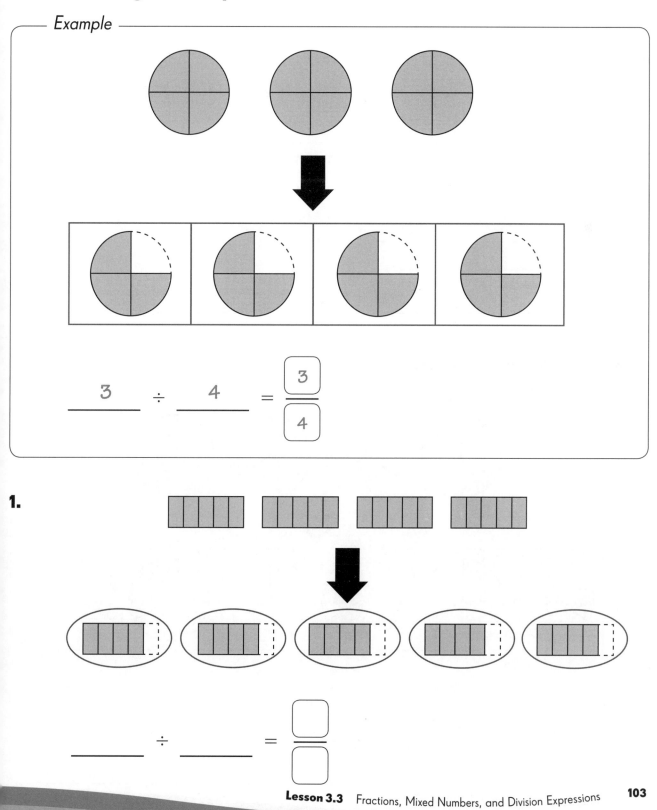

Example

$$\underline{} \div \underline{} = \frac{3}{4}$$

3 ÷ 4

1.

$$\underline{} \div \underline{} = \frac{\boxed{}}{\boxed{}}$$

Write each division expression as a fraction.

2.

$$5 \div 7 = \frac{\boxed{}}{\boxed{}}$$

3.

$$3 \div 10 = \frac{\boxed{}}{\boxed{}}$$

4.

$$4 \div 9 = \frac{\boxed{}}{\boxed{}}$$

5.

$$2 \div 11 = \frac{\boxed{}}{\boxed{}}$$

Write each fraction as a division expression.

Example

$$\frac{7}{8} = \underline{\quad 7 \quad} \div \underline{\quad 8 \quad}$$

6. $\dfrac{5}{12} = \underline{\qquad} \div \underline{\qquad}$

7. $\dfrac{1}{10} = \underline{\qquad} \div \underline{\qquad}$

8. $\dfrac{6}{7} = \underline{\qquad} \div \underline{\qquad}$

Look at the diagram. Complete.

Example

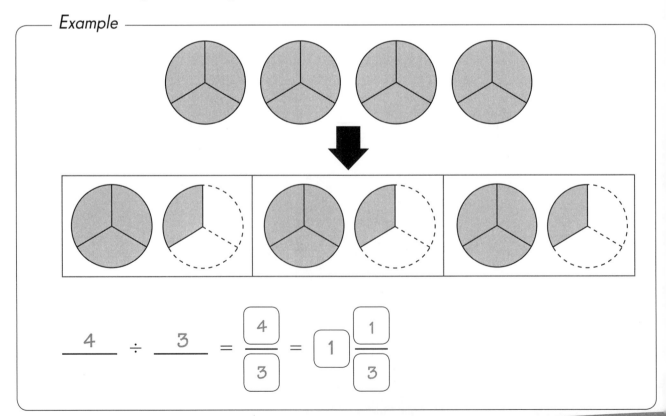

$$\underline{\quad 4 \quad} \div \underline{\quad 3 \quad} = \frac{\boxed{4}}{\boxed{3}} = \boxed{1}\frac{\boxed{1}}{\boxed{3}}$$

Look at the diagram. Complete.

9.

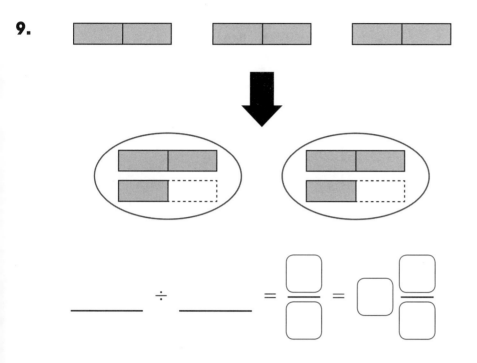

$$\underline{\hspace{2cm}} \div \underline{\hspace{2cm}} = \frac{\boxed{}}{\boxed{}} = \boxed{}\frac{\boxed{}}{\boxed{}}$$

Complete.

10.

$$7 \div 4 = \frac{\boxed{}}{\boxed{}}$$

$$= \frac{\boxed{}}{\boxed{}} + \frac{\boxed{}}{\boxed{}}$$

$$= 1 + \frac{\boxed{}}{\boxed{}}$$

$$= \boxed{}\frac{\boxed{}}{\boxed{}}$$

11.

$$35 \div 11 = \frac{\boxed{}}{\boxed{}}$$

$$= \frac{\boxed{}}{\boxed{}} + \frac{\boxed{}}{\boxed{}}$$

$$= 3 + \frac{\boxed{}}{\boxed{}}$$

$$= \boxed{}\frac{\boxed{}}{\boxed{}}$$

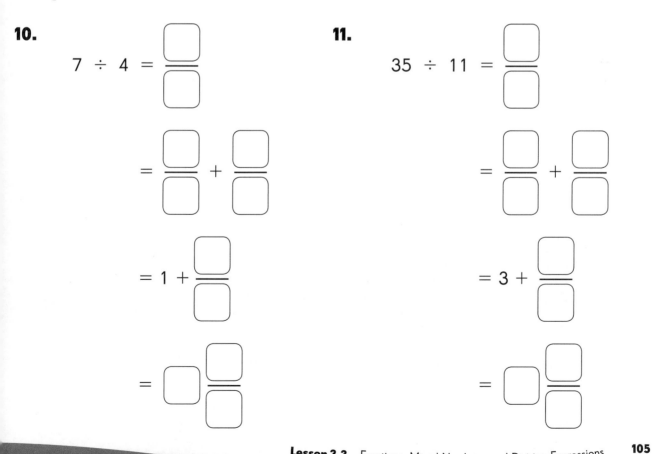

Divide. Express each quotient as a mixed number.

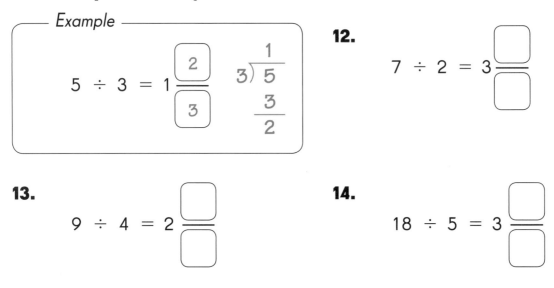

12.

$7 \div 2 = 3\dfrac{\Box}{\Box}$

13.

$9 \div 4 = 2\dfrac{\Box}{\Box}$

14.

$18 \div 5 = 3\dfrac{\Box}{\Box}$

Write each fraction in simplest form. Then divide to express each quotient as a mixed number.

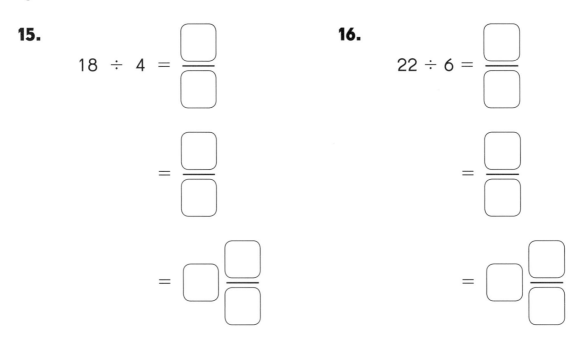

Practice 4   Expressing Fractions, Division Expressions, and Mixed Numbers as Decimals

Write each fraction as a decimal.

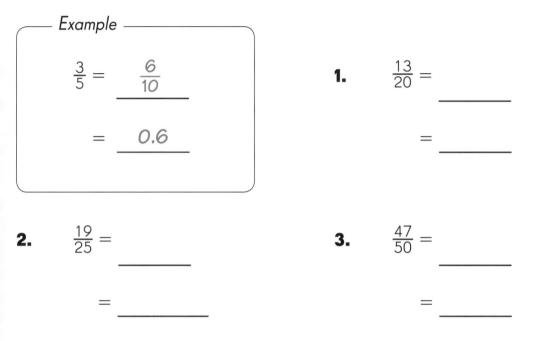

Example

$\frac{3}{5} = \frac{6}{10}$

$= 0.6$

1. $\frac{13}{20} =$ _____

   $=$ _____

2. $\frac{19}{25} =$ _____

   $=$ _____

3. $\frac{47}{50} =$ _____

   $=$ _____

Express each division expression as a mixed number in simplest form and as a decimal.

	Division expression	Express division expression as	
		a mixed number	a decimal
4.	$7 \div 2$		
5.	$9 \div 4$		
6.	$21 \div 5$		
7.	$101 \div 25$		

Express each improper fraction as a decimal.

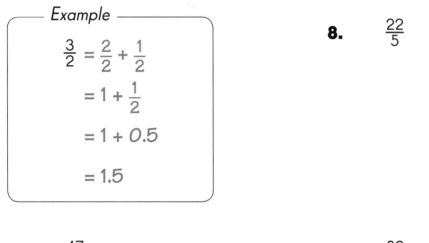

Example

$$\frac{3}{2} = \frac{2}{2} + \frac{1}{2}$$
$$= 1 + \frac{1}{2}$$
$$= 1 + 0.5$$
$$= 1.5$$

8. $\frac{22}{5}$

9. $\frac{47}{20}$

10. $\frac{32}{25}$

Solve. Show your work.

11.   A coil of rope 603 feet long is cut into 25 equal pieces. What is the length of each piece? Express your answer as a mixed number and as a decimal.

Practice 5   Adding Mixed Numbers

Add. Express each sum in simplest form.

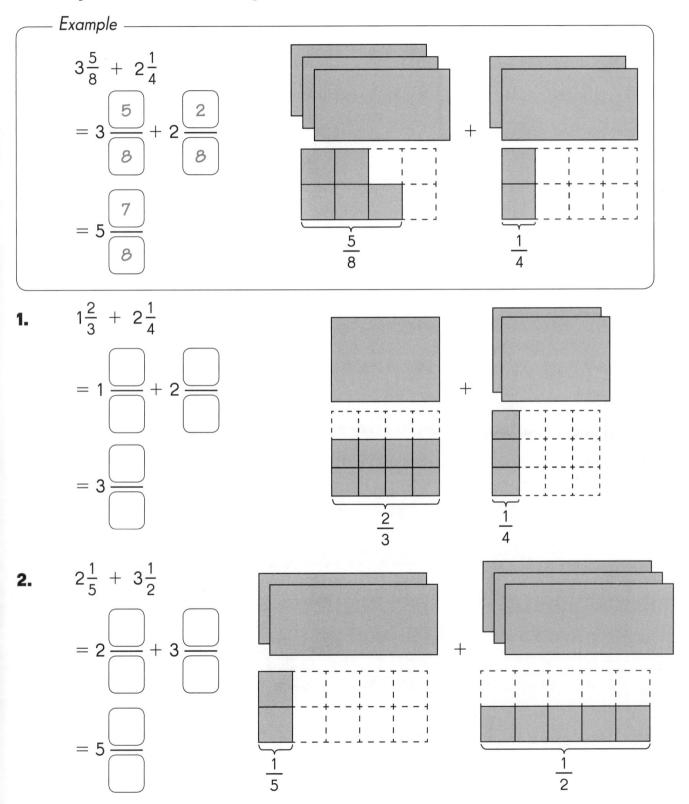

Example

$$3\frac{5}{8} + 2\frac{1}{4}$$

$$= 3\frac{\boxed{5}}{\boxed{8}} + 2\frac{\boxed{2}}{\boxed{8}}$$

$$= 5\frac{\boxed{7}}{\boxed{8}}$$

$$\frac{5}{8} \qquad \frac{1}{4}$$

1. $1\frac{2}{3} + 2\frac{1}{4}$

$$= 1\frac{\boxed{}}{\boxed{}} + 2\frac{\boxed{}}{\boxed{}}$$

$$= 3\frac{\boxed{}}{\boxed{}}$$

$$\frac{2}{3} \qquad \frac{1}{4}$$

2. $2\frac{1}{5} + 3\frac{1}{2}$

$$= 2\frac{\boxed{}}{\boxed{}} + 3\frac{\boxed{}}{\boxed{}}$$

$$= 5\frac{\boxed{}}{\boxed{}}$$

$$\frac{1}{5} \qquad \frac{1}{2}$$

Add. Express each sum in simplest form.

3. $3\frac{2}{7} + 2\frac{5}{14}$

4. $5\frac{7}{12} + 3\frac{1}{4}$

5. $4\frac{1}{15} + 1\frac{3}{10}$

6. $12\frac{1}{9} + 9\frac{5}{6}$

Add. Express each sum in simplest form.

7. $1\frac{4}{5} + 2\frac{1}{3}$

$= 1\frac{\boxed{}}{\boxed{}} + 2\frac{\boxed{}}{\boxed{}}$

$= 3\frac{\boxed{}}{\boxed{}}$

$= 4\frac{\boxed{}}{\boxed{}}$

$\frac{4}{5}$ $+$ $\frac{1}{3}$

Add. Express each sum in simplest form.

8. $3\frac{5}{12} + 1\frac{2}{3}$

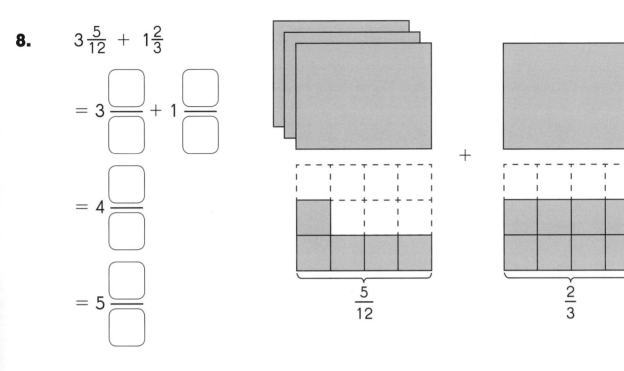

$= 3\dfrac{\boxed{}}{\boxed{}} + 1\dfrac{\boxed{}}{\boxed{}}$

$= 4\dfrac{\boxed{}}{\boxed{}}$

$= 5\dfrac{\boxed{}}{\boxed{}}$

$\dfrac{5}{12}$ $+$ $\dfrac{2}{3}$

9. $2\frac{3}{4} + 3\frac{2}{5}$

10. $2\frac{5}{9} + 1\frac{5}{6}$

11. $7\frac{8}{9} + 9\frac{5}{12}$

12. $5\frac{7}{12} + 1\frac{3}{4}$

Use benchmarks to estimate each sum.

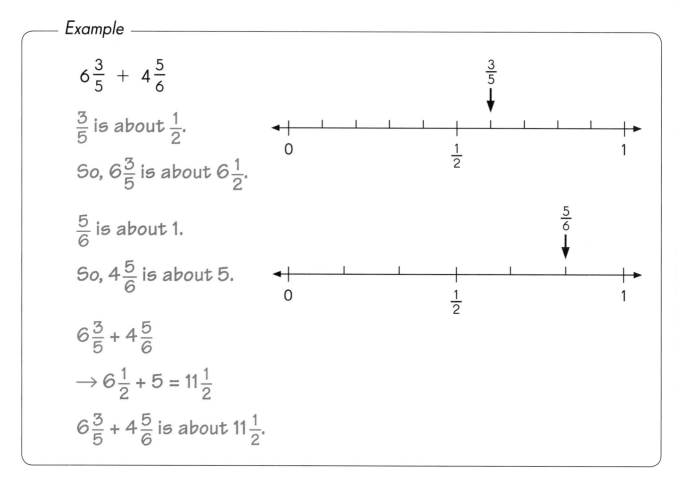

Example

$6\frac{3}{5} + 4\frac{5}{6}$

$\frac{3}{5}$ is about $\frac{1}{2}$.

So, $6\frac{3}{5}$ is about $6\frac{1}{2}$.

$\frac{5}{6}$ is about 1.

So, $4\frac{5}{6}$ is about 5.

$6\frac{3}{5} + 4\frac{5}{6}$

$\rightarrow 6\frac{1}{2} + 5 = 11\frac{1}{2}$

$6\frac{3}{5} + 4\frac{5}{6}$ is about $11\frac{1}{2}$.

13. $9\frac{6}{7} + 7\frac{5}{12}$

14. $4\frac{7}{12} + 10\frac{1}{9}$

Practice 6 Subtracting Mixed Numbers

Subtract. Express each difference in simplest form.

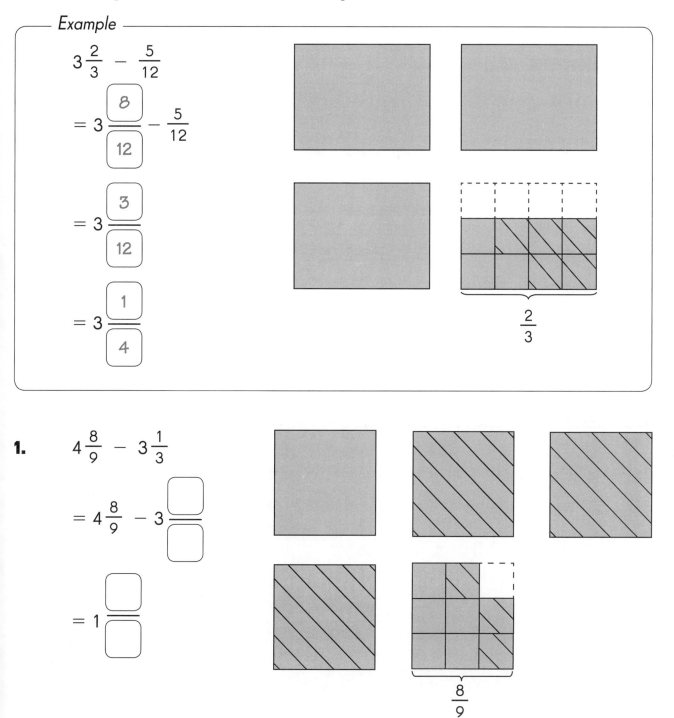

Example

$$3\frac{2}{3} - \frac{5}{12}$$

$$= 3\frac{\boxed{8}}{\boxed{12}} - \frac{5}{12}$$

$$= 3\frac{\boxed{3}}{\boxed{12}}$$

$$= 3\frac{\boxed{1}}{\boxed{4}}$$

$\frac{2}{3}$

1. $4\frac{8}{9} - 3\frac{1}{3}$

$$= 4\frac{8}{9} - 3\frac{\boxed{}}{\boxed{}}$$

$$= 1\frac{\boxed{}}{\boxed{}}$$

$\frac{8}{9}$

Subtract. Express each difference in simplest form.

2. $3\frac{7}{12} - 2\frac{3}{8}$

$= 3\dfrac{\boxed{}}{\boxed{}} - 2\dfrac{\boxed{}}{\boxed{}}$

$= 1\dfrac{\boxed{}}{\boxed{}}$

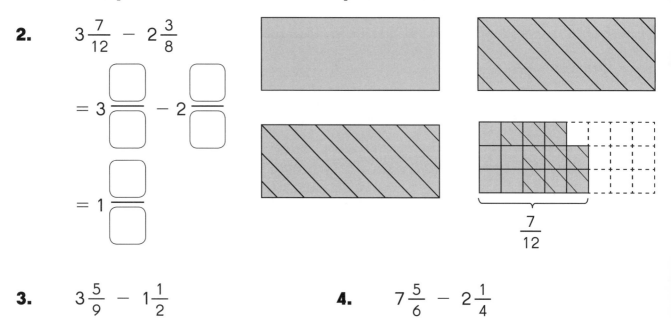

$\dfrac{7}{12}$

3. $3\frac{5}{9} - 1\frac{1}{2}$

4. $7\frac{5}{6} - 2\frac{1}{4}$

Subtract. Express each difference as a mixed number.

5. $3\frac{1}{4} - 1\frac{7}{8}$

$= 3\dfrac{\boxed{}}{\boxed{}} - 1\frac{7}{8}$

$= \boxed{}\dfrac{\boxed{}}{\boxed{}} - \boxed{}\dfrac{\boxed{}}{\boxed{}}$

$= \boxed{}\dfrac{\boxed{}}{\boxed{}}$

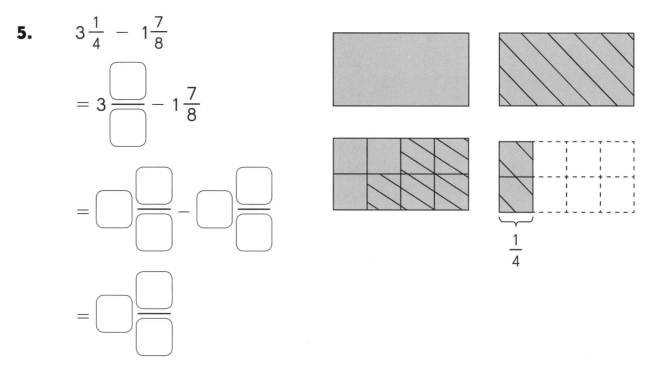

$\dfrac{1}{4}$

Name: _____   **Date:** _____

Subtract. Express each difference as a mixed number.

6. $5\dfrac{1}{3} \ - \ 3\dfrac{5}{12}$

$= 5\dfrac{\boxed{}}{\boxed{}} - 3\dfrac{5}{12}$

$= \boxed{}\,\dfrac{\boxed{}}{\boxed{}} - \boxed{}\,\dfrac{\boxed{}}{\boxed{}}$

$= \boxed{}\,\dfrac{\boxed{}}{\boxed{}}$

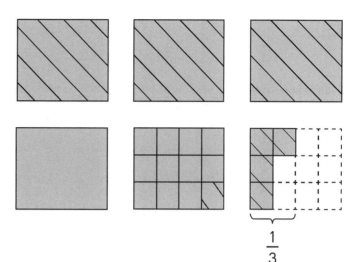

$\underbrace{}_{\dfrac{1}{3}}$

7. $4\dfrac{1}{5} \ - \ 1\dfrac{1}{3}$ **8.** $6\dfrac{3}{8} \ - \ 3\dfrac{5}{6}$

9. $7\dfrac{1}{4} \ - \ 5\dfrac{11}{12}$ **10.** $8\dfrac{1}{3} \ - \ 4\dfrac{3}{4}$

Use benchmarks to estimate each difference.

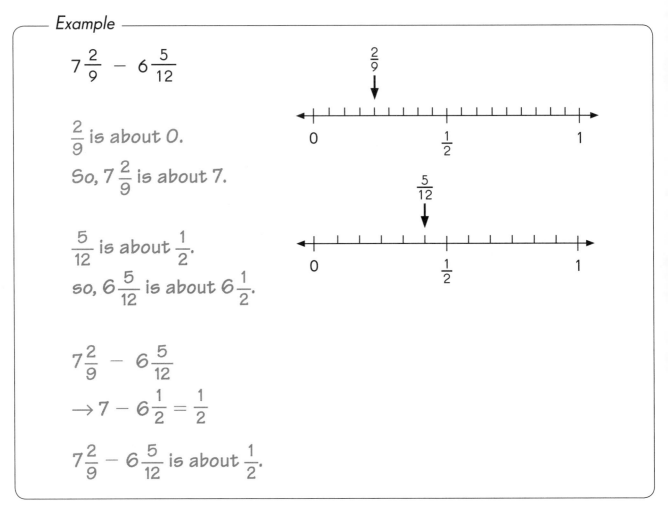

Example

$7\frac{2}{9} - 6\frac{5}{12}$

$\frac{2}{9}$ is about 0.

So, $7\frac{2}{9}$ is about 7.

$\frac{5}{12}$ is about $\frac{1}{2}$.

so, $6\frac{5}{12}$ is about $6\frac{1}{2}$.

$7\frac{2}{9} - 6\frac{5}{12}$

$\rightarrow 7 - 6\frac{1}{2} = \frac{1}{2}$

$7\frac{2}{9} - 6\frac{5}{12}$ is about $\frac{1}{2}$.

11. $\quad 12\frac{2}{5} - 8\frac{7}{12}$

12. $\quad 20\frac{1}{8} - 5\frac{3}{9}$

Practice 7   Real-World Problems: Fractions and Mixed Numbers

Solve. Show your work.

1.   Elena has 12 pieces of banana bread. She gives an equal amount of banana bread to 5 friends. How many pieces of banana bread does she give each friend?

2.   A utility bill shows that a household used 2,001 gallons of water in a 5-day period. What was the average amount of water used by the household each day?

3.   A ball of string is 50 yards long. A shipper uses 5 yards of string to tie packages. The remaining string is then cut into 7 equal pieces. What is the length of each of the 7 pieces of string?

Solve. Show your work.

4.   Steve picks 55 pounds of pears. He packs an equal amount
      of pears into 6 bags. He then has 4 pounds of pears left.
      What is the weight of pears in each bag?

5.   Jeremy puts an empty container under a leaking faucet. In the
      first hour, $\frac{3}{8}$ quart of water collects. In the second hour,
      $\frac{1}{6}$ quart of water collects. How much water collects in the
      container in the two hours?

Solve. Show your work.

6. Arnold buys $\frac{8}{9}$ pound of ground turkey. He uses $\frac{3}{4}$ pound of the ground turkey to make meatballs. How many pounds of ground turkey are left?

7. A snail is at the bottom of a well. In the first 10 minutes, the snail climbs $23\frac{7}{12}$ inches. In the next 10 minutes, it climbs $19\frac{5}{6}$ inches. How far is the snail from the bottom of the well after 20 minutes?

Solve. Show your work.

8.   Johnny is jogging along a track. He has already jogged $1\frac{2}{3}$ miles.
      He plans to jog a total of $3\frac{1}{4}$ miles. How many miles does
      he have left to jog?

Practice 8   Real-World Problems: Fractions and Mixed Numbers

Solve. Show your work.

1. Susanne and Barry each buy 4 equal-sized bagels. They divide the bagels equally among themselves and 3 other friends. How many bagels does each person get?

2. Maya has 5 sheets of paper. She cuts each sheet into 3 equal-sized rectangles. The rectangles are shared equally among 6 students. How many rectangles does each student get?

Solve. Show your work.

3.   Mrs. Quirk buys 1 quart of milk. Michael drinks $\frac{2}{7}$ quart of it.

       Joel drinks $\frac{1}{3}$ quart of it. How many quarts of milk are left?

Solve. Show your work.

4.   An organic farmer buys a piece of land. She plants tomatoes

on $\frac{5}{9}$ of the land and green beans on $\frac{1}{12}$ of the land.

She plants potatoes on the remaining piece of land.

What fraction of the land does she plant with potatoes?

Solve. Show your work.

5.   A package contains three types of bagels, plain, wheat, and sesame. The weight of the plain bagels is $1\frac{2}{3}$ pounds. The weight of the wheat bagels is $2\frac{5}{6}$ pounds. The total weight of the three types of bagels is 5 pounds. What is the weight of the sesame bagels?

Solve. Show your work.

6. Reggie and Jay go for a walk every morning. Reggie walks $2\frac{1}{4}$ miles. Jay walks $1\frac{3}{8}$ miles less than Reggie. What is the total distance they walk every morning?

Solve. Show your work.

7.   Alicia uses $\frac{3}{4}$ gallon of paint to paint her room. Becca uses $\frac{4}{5}$ gallon more than Alicia to paint her room. How many gallons of paint do they use altogether?

Solve. Show your work.

8. A monkey climbs $3\frac{3}{5}$ feet up a coconut tree that has a height
of 10 feet. It rests for a while and continues to climb another
$4\frac{2}{3}$ feet up the tree. How many more feet must the monkey climb to
reach the top of the tree?

Math Journal

$$\frac{1}{8} + \frac{2}{3} = ?$$

Draw a model, and explain the steps you can use to add $\frac{2}{3}$ to $\frac{1}{8}$.

Put On Your Thinking Cap!

Challenging Practice

Solve. Show your work.

Tina, Troy and Nate had a total of 25 equal-sized square tiles to place over a square grid. Tina used $\frac{8}{25}$ of the square tiles. Troy used $\frac{1}{5}$ of the square tiles. Shade the square grid below to show how Tina and Troy could have placed the square tiles. What fraction of the square grid must Nate place the tiles on so that $\frac{1}{5}$ of the square grid is **not** covered?

Put On Your Thinking Cap!

Problem Solving

Solve. Use a model to help you.

Paul mixes cement with sand. He uses $3\frac{3}{4}$ kilograms of cement and $\frac{1}{2}$ kilogram more sand than cement. He needs 10 kilograms of the mixture. Does he have enough mixture? If yes, how much more does he have and if no, how much more does he need?

Chapter 4 Multiplying and Dividing Fractions and Mixed Numbers

Practice 1   Multiplying Proper Fractions

Complete.

1.

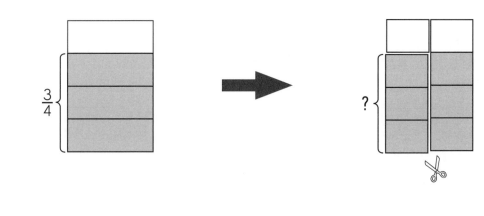

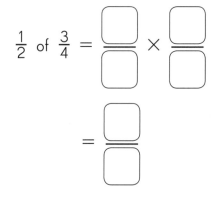

$\frac{1}{2}$ of $\frac{3}{4}$ = $\dfrac{\Box}{\Box}$ × $\dfrac{\Box}{\Box}$

= $\dfrac{\Box}{\Box}$

Multiply. Express the product in simplest form.

2. $\frac{3}{8} \times \frac{1}{2} =$

3. $\frac{5}{12} \times \frac{7}{8} =$

Multiply. Express the product in simplest form.

4. $\frac{2}{11} \times \frac{7}{12} = \frac{14}{132}$

5. $\frac{3}{8} \times \frac{4}{9} = \frac{12}{72}$

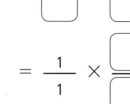

Complete. Express the product in simplest form.

6. $\frac{1}{3}$ of $\frac{5}{8} = \dfrac{\boxed{}}{\boxed{}} \times \dfrac{\boxed{}}{\boxed{}}$

$= \dfrac{\boxed{}}{\boxed{}}$

7. $\frac{2}{7}$ of $\frac{9}{11} = \dfrac{\boxed{}}{\boxed{}} \times \dfrac{\boxed{}}{\boxed{}}$

$= \dfrac{\boxed{}}{\boxed{}}$

8. $\frac{2}{5}$ of $\frac{7}{10} = \dfrac{\boxed{}}{\boxed{}} \times \dfrac{\boxed{}}{\boxed{}}$

$= \dfrac{1}{\boxed{}} \times \dfrac{\boxed{}}{\boxed{}}$

$= \dfrac{1 \times \boxed{}}{\boxed{} \times \boxed{}}$

$= \dfrac{\boxed{}}{\boxed{}}$

9. $\frac{3}{4}$ of $\frac{8}{9} = \dfrac{\boxed{}}{\boxed{}} \times \dfrac{\boxed{}}{\boxed{}}$

$= \dfrac{1}{\boxed{}} \times \dfrac{\boxed{}}{\boxed{}}$

$= \dfrac{1}{1} \times \dfrac{\boxed{}}{\boxed{}}$

$= \dfrac{\boxed{}}{\boxed{}}$

Practice 2 Real-World Problems: Multiplying with Proper Fractions

Solve. Draw models to help you.

1. Lena has some eggs. She uses $\frac{3}{5}$ of the eggs to make waffles and

scrambled eggs. She uses $\frac{2}{3}$ of the eggs she took to make waffles.

What fraction of the total number of eggs does Lena use to

make waffles?

2. Dawn has $\frac{5}{6}$ yard of lace. She uses $\frac{4}{5}$ of it for a dress and the rest for

a jewel box. How much lace does she use for the jewel box?

Solve. Show your work.

3. Tasha finished a job in $\frac{3}{4}$ hour. Megan finished it in $\frac{4}{5}$ of the time Tasha took. How long did Megan take to finish the job?

4. Lily has a bottle containing $\frac{7}{8}$ quart of milk. She pours $\frac{4}{5}$ of it into a bowl. What amount of milk does she pour into the bowl?

5. Raul ran $\frac{3}{4}$ mile in a race. Eduardo ran $\frac{2}{7}$ of the distance that Raul ran. What distance did Eduardo run?

Solve. Draw models to help you.

6. Jenny spends $\frac{1}{6}$ of her paycheck and saves $\frac{2}{5}$ of the remaining amount. What fraction of her total paycheck is saved?

Solve. Draw models to help you.

7. In Rod's family, $\frac{3}{4}$ of the members wear glasses. Of those who do not wear glasses, $\frac{1}{3}$ are male. What fraction of the family are males who do not wear glasses?

Solve. Draw models to help you.

8. Ned folded a set of origami figures. Of this set, $\frac{5}{8}$ are cranes
and $\frac{1}{6}$ of the remainder are frogs. The rest are grasshoppers.
What fraction of the origami figures are grasshoppers?

Solve. Show your work.

9. In a garden, $\frac{2}{3}$ of the flowers are roses. Of the roses in the garden, $\frac{5}{12}$ are yellow and the rest are red. What fraction of the flowers are red roses?

10. Karen collects local and foreign coins. Of the coins in her collection, $\frac{1}{4}$ are foreign coins. Of the foreign coins, $\frac{2}{5}$ are from Mexico. What fraction of the collection are foreign coins that are not from Mexico?

Practice 3   Multiplying Improper Fractions by Fractions

Complete.

1.

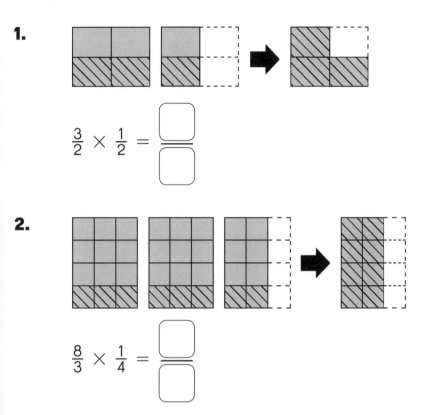

$$\frac{3}{2} \times \frac{1}{2} = \frac{\boxed{}}{\boxed{}}$$

2.

$$\frac{8}{3} \times \frac{1}{4} = \frac{\boxed{}}{\boxed{}}$$

Find the product.

3.

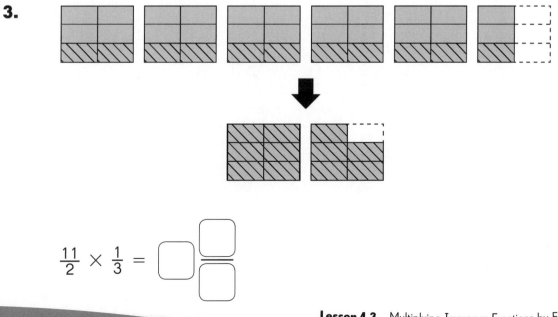

$$\frac{11}{2} \times \frac{1}{3} = \boxed{}\,\frac{\boxed{}}{\boxed{}}$$

Multiply. Express the product in simplest form.

Example

$$\frac{4}{5} \times \frac{7}{6}$$

Method 1

$$\frac{4}{5} \times \frac{7}{6} = \frac{4 \div 2}{5} \times \frac{7}{6 \div 2}$$

$$= \frac{2}{5} \times \frac{7}{3}$$

$$= \frac{2 \times 7}{5 \times 3}$$

$$= \frac{14}{15}$$

Method 2

$$\frac{4}{5} \times \frac{7}{6} = \frac{4 \times 7}{5 \times 6}$$

$$= \frac{28}{30}$$

$$= \frac{28 \div 2}{30 \div 2}$$

$$= \frac{14}{15}$$

4. $\dfrac{7}{4} \times \dfrac{1}{3} =$

5. $\dfrac{9}{8} \times \dfrac{2}{7} =$

6. $\dfrac{8}{3} \times \dfrac{3}{10} =$

7. $\dfrac{15}{9} \times \dfrac{3}{20} =$

Multiply. Express the product as a whole number or a mixed number in simplest form.

Example

$\dfrac{2}{5} \times \dfrac{15}{4}$

Method 1

$\dfrac{2}{5} \times \dfrac{15}{4} = \dfrac{2 \div 2}{5} \times \dfrac{15}{4 \div 2}$

$= \dfrac{1}{5 \div 5} \times \dfrac{15 \div 5}{2}$

$= \dfrac{1 \times 3}{1 \times 2}$

$= \dfrac{3}{2}$

$= 1\dfrac{1}{2}$

Method 2

$\dfrac{2}{5} \times \dfrac{15}{4} = \dfrac{2 \times 15}{5 \times 4}$

$= \dfrac{30}{20}$

$= \dfrac{3}{2}$

$= 1\dfrac{1}{2}$

---

8. $\dfrac{3}{4} \times \dfrac{8}{6} =$

9. $\dfrac{16}{7} \times \dfrac{21}{2} =$

10. $\dfrac{15}{12} \times \dfrac{8}{5} =$

11. $\dfrac{32}{9} \times \dfrac{36}{8} =$

Multiply. Express the product as a whole number or a mixed number in simplest form.

12. $\dfrac{7}{8} \times \dfrac{6}{5} =$

13. $\dfrac{11}{12} \times \dfrac{28}{3} =$

14. $\dfrac{21}{5} \times \dfrac{15}{6} =$

15. $\dfrac{25}{4} \times \dfrac{18}{10} =$

16. $\dfrac{30}{9} \times \dfrac{7}{2} =$

17. $\dfrac{14}{8} \times \dfrac{5}{3} =$

Practice 4   Multiplying Mixed Numbers and Whole Numbers

Complete.

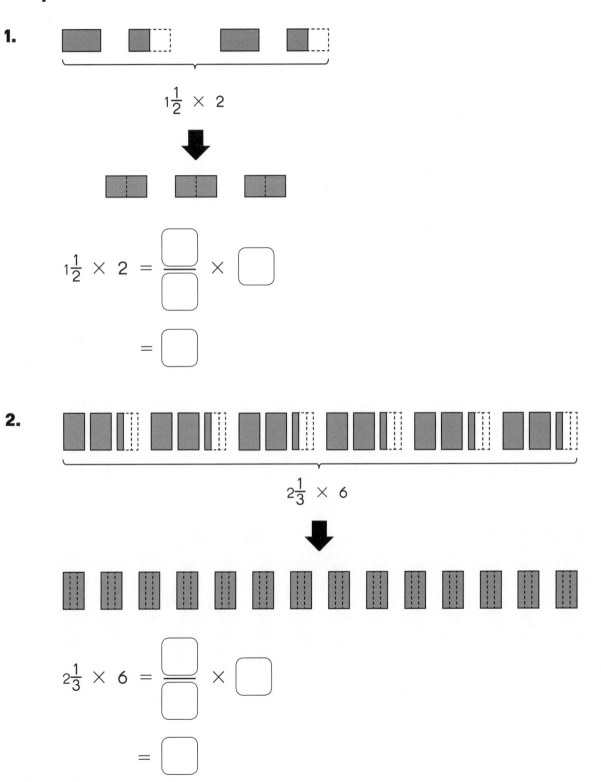

1.

$1\frac{1}{2} \times 2$

$1\frac{1}{2} \times 2 = \dfrac{\boxed{}}{\boxed{}} \times \boxed{}$

$= \boxed{}$

2.

$2\frac{1}{3} \times 6$

$2\frac{1}{3} \times 6 = \dfrac{\boxed{}}{\boxed{}} \times \boxed{}$

$= \boxed{}$

Multiply. Express the product as a whole number or a mixed number in simplest form.

> *Example*
>
> $$9 \times 2\frac{1}{3}$$
>
> $$9 \times 2\frac{1}{3} = 9 \times \frac{7}{3}$$
>
> $$= \frac{9 \times 7}{3}$$
>
> $$= \frac{63}{3}$$
>
> $$= 21$$

3. $4\frac{1}{5} \times 15 =$

4. $2\frac{3}{7} \times 28 =$

5. $24 \times 1\frac{5}{6} =$

6. $4\frac{1}{2} \times 18 =$

**Multiply. Express the product as a whole number or a
mixed number in simplest form.**

7. $2\frac{3}{4} \times 16 =$

8. $32 \times 3\frac{1}{8} =$

**Multiply. Express the product as a whole number or a
mixed number in simplest form.**

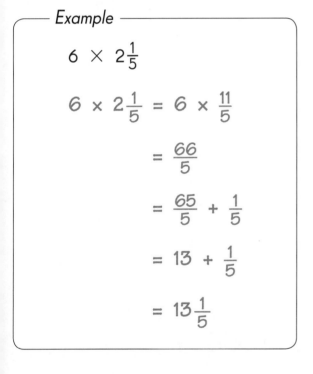

Example

$6 \times 2\frac{1}{5}$

$6 \times 2\frac{1}{5} = 6 \times \frac{11}{5}$

$= \frac{66}{5}$

$= \frac{65}{5} + \frac{1}{5}$

$= 13 + \frac{1}{5}$

$= 13\frac{1}{5}$

9. $4 \times 2\frac{7}{9} =$

10. $5 \times 2\frac{3}{7} =$

Multiply. Express the product as a whole number or a mixed number in simplest form.

11. $2\frac{1}{4} \times 7 =$

12. $8\frac{3}{4} \times 2 =$

13. $1\frac{4}{5} \times 12 =$

14. $12 \times 2\frac{3}{8} =$

15. $21 \times 2\frac{5}{9} =$

16. $26 \times 1\frac{1}{6} =$

Practice 5 Real-World Problems: Multiplying Mixed Numbers

Solve. Show your work.

1. At a party, there are 8 guests. Each guest eats $2\frac{1}{4}$ oranges.

   How many oranges do the 8 guests eat?

   1 guest $\longrightarrow$ $2\frac{1}{4}$ oranges

   8 guests $\longrightarrow$ _____ $\times$ _____ oranges

   $=$ _____

   The 8 guests eat a total of _____ oranges.

2. One pound of chicken costs \$3. Jim buys $8\frac{2}{3}$ pounds of chicken.

   How much does Jim pay for the chicken?

3. The length of a picture is 2 yards and its width is $1\frac{2}{5}$ yards. Find the

   area of the picture. Express your answer as a decimal.

Solve. Show your work.

4.   Sue buys 5 pieces of fabric. Each piece of fabric is $1\frac{7}{10}$ yards long.

   a.   What is the total length of the fabric she buys?

   b.   One yard of the fabric costs $5. How much does she pay for all 5 pieces of fabric?

5.   Angela works $1\frac{1}{2}$ hours a day and is paid $7 per hour. She works 5 days a week. How much does Angela earn in 7 weeks?

Name: _____   Date: _____

Practice 6   Dividing a Fraction by a Whole Number

**Shade parts of the model to show the division expression.
Then complete.**

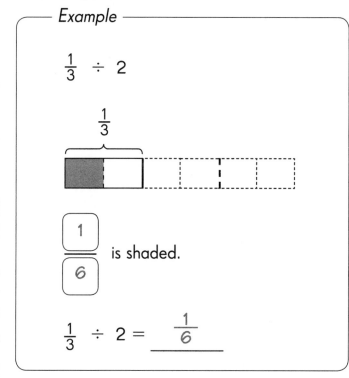

> **Example**
>
> $\frac{1}{3} \div 2$
>
> $\frac{1}{3}$
>
> $\boxed{\dfrac{1}{6}}$ is shaded.
>
> $\frac{1}{3} \div 2 = \underline{\ \frac{1}{6}\ }$

1. $\frac{1}{6} \div 3$

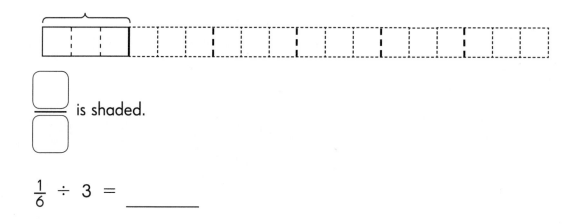

$\boxed{\dfrac{}{}}$ is shaded.

$\frac{1}{6} \div 3 = \underline{\hspace{1.5cm}}$

Divide. Draw models to help you.

2. $\dfrac{4}{5} \div 2 =$

3. $\dfrac{6}{7} \div 3 =$

4. $\dfrac{3}{4} \div 2 =$

5. $\dfrac{2}{5} \div 3 =$

Divide. Express each quotient in simplest form.

6. $\dfrac{4}{5} \div 7 =$

7. $\dfrac{5}{8} \div 9 =$

8. $\dfrac{8}{9} \div 4 =$

9. $\dfrac{10}{11} \div 5 =$

Solve. Show your work.

10.   Mr. Chagall's garden covers $\frac{2}{5}$ of an acre of land. He divides the land into 4 equal sections. What fraction of an acre is each section of the garden?

11.   Gordon pours $\frac{4}{9}$ quart of milk from a pitcher equally into 4 mugs.

   a.   Find the amount of milk in each mug.

   b.   Find the amount of milk in 3 mugs.

Solve. Show your work.

12. Calvin buys $\frac{3}{5}$ pound of ground beef. He divides the beef into 6 equal portions.

    a. Find the weight of 1 portion of beef.

    b. Find the weight of 4 portions of beef.

13. Devon buys a plot of land with an area of $\frac{5}{6}$ square kilometer.

    He divides the land equally into 4 smaller plots. What is the total area of 3 of the smaller plots of land?

Practice 7 Real-World Problems: Multiplying and Dividing with Fractions

Solve. Draw models to help you.

1. Evan typed 72 pages of notes one day. He typed $\frac{1}{2}$ of the pages in the morning and $\frac{1}{3}$ of the pages in the afternoon. He typed the rest of the pages in the evening. How many pages of notes did he type in the morning and afternoon?

2. Last Saturday, Jay spent 6 hours playing games, studying and talking with his friends. He spent $\frac{2}{5}$ of the time playing games and $\frac{1}{2}$ of the time studying. How many minutes did he spend talking with his friends?

Solve. Draw models to help you.

3. Joanne earns $720 a week. She spends $\frac{1}{3}$ of her money on groceries and household goods and $\frac{3}{4}$ of the remaining money on rent. How much money does she spend on rent, groceries and household goods?

4. During a triathlon, Sharon swims $\frac{1}{4}$ of the total route and cycles $\frac{3}{5}$ of the remaining route. She runs the rest of the route. If she runs 3,600 meters, find the total distance of the triathlon route.

Solve. Show your work.

5.   Victoria has a 2-pound package of flour. She uses $\frac{2}{5}$ of the flour to make a pizza. She then uses $\frac{3}{10}$ of the remaining flour to make bread. Find the weight of the package of flour that she has left. Express your answer as a decimal.

Solve. Show your work.

6. Karen collects $\frac{6}{7}$ quart of rainwater. She uses $\frac{1}{2}$ of the water to clean her bicycle and uses the remaining water equally for 3 houseplants. What volume of water does she use for each houseplant?

7. Ricardo spends $\frac{8}{9}$ hour reading the newspaper. He spends $\frac{1}{4}$ of the time reading the world news and splits the remaining time equally between the sports news and the comics. How much time does he spend reading the comics?

Math Journal

Rachel drew a model to solve this problem:

Earl pours $\frac{1}{3}$ of a bottle of juice into his glass. Roberto pours $\frac{1}{3}$ of the remainder into his glass. What fraction of the bottle of juice is left?

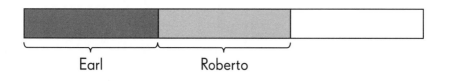

Earl   Roberto

$1 - \frac{1}{3} - \frac{1}{3} = \frac{1}{3}$

$\frac{1}{3}$ of the bottle of juice is left.

Did Rachel solve the problem correctly? Explain.

Put On Your Thinking Cap!

Challenging Practice

An art teacher has a box of markers. She keeps half of the markers in the box and gives $\frac{1}{3}$ of the other half to group A. The remaining markers were shared equally among the 8 students in group B. What fraction of the whole box does each of the students in group B get?

Put On Your Thinking Cap!

Problem Solving

Mimi's Market sold 24 heads of lettuce one morning. That afternoon $\frac{2}{7}$ of the remaining heads of lettuce were sold. The number of heads left was now $\frac{1}{2}$ of the number the market had at the beginning of the day. How many heads of lettuce were there at the beginning of the day?

Cumulative Review

for Chapters 3 and 4

Concepts and Skills

Shade and label the model to show the sum of $\frac{1}{3}$ and $\frac{3}{5}$.
Then complete the addition sentence. *(Lesson 3.1)*

1.

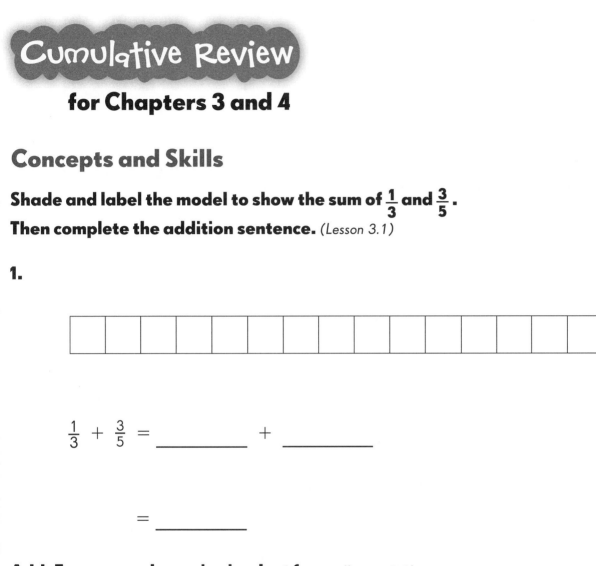

$\frac{1}{3}$ + $\frac{3}{5}$ = _____ + _____

= _____

Add. Express each sum in simplest form. *(Lesson 3.1)*

2. $\frac{3}{4}$ + $\frac{1}{12}$ =

3. $\frac{3}{5}$ + $\frac{2}{7}$ =

Estimate each sum by using the benchmarks, 0, $\frac{1}{2}$ or 1. *(Lesson 3.1)*

4. $\frac{8}{9} + \frac{2}{5}$

5. $\frac{1}{8} + \frac{6}{7} + \frac{1}{6}$

Shade and label the model to show the difference between $\frac{4}{5}$ and $\frac{2}{3}$. Then complete the subtraction sentence. *(Lesson 3.2)*

6.

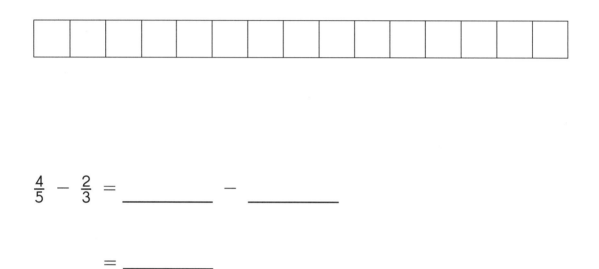

$\frac{4}{5} - \frac{2}{3} =$ _____ $-$ _____

$=$ _____

Subtract. Express each difference in simplest form. *(Lesson 3.2)*

7. $\frac{3}{4} - \frac{1}{12} =$

8. $\frac{3}{5} - \frac{3}{9} =$

Name: _____ **Date:** _____

Estimate each difference by using the benchmarks, 0, $\frac{1}{2}$ or 1. *(Lesson 3.2)*

9. $\quad \frac{4}{5} - \frac{3}{8}$

10. $\quad \frac{7}{12} - \frac{5}{9}$

Write each division expression as a fraction. *(Lesson 3.3)*

11. $\quad 4 \div 9 = \dfrac{\boxed{}}{\boxed{}}$

12. $\quad 8 \div 11 = \dfrac{\boxed{}}{\boxed{}}$

Write each fraction as a division expression. *(Lesson 3.3)*

13. $\quad \frac{5}{6} = $ _____ $\div$ _____

14. $\quad \frac{7}{12} = $ _____ $\div$ _____

Complete. *(Lesson 3.3)*

15. $\quad 7 \div 5 = \dfrac{\boxed{}}{\boxed{}}$

$\qquad = \dfrac{\boxed{}}{\boxed{}} + \dfrac{\boxed{}}{\boxed{}}$

$\qquad = 1 + \dfrac{\boxed{}}{\boxed{}}$

$\qquad = \boxed{} \dfrac{\boxed{}}{\boxed{}}$

16. $\quad 19 \div 4 = \dfrac{\boxed{}}{\boxed{}}$

$\qquad = \dfrac{\boxed{}}{\boxed{}} + \dfrac{\boxed{}}{\boxed{}}$

$\qquad = 4 + \dfrac{\boxed{}}{\boxed{}}$

$\qquad = \boxed{} \dfrac{\boxed{}}{\boxed{}}$

Divide. Express each quotient as a mixed number in simplest form. *(Lesson 3.3)*

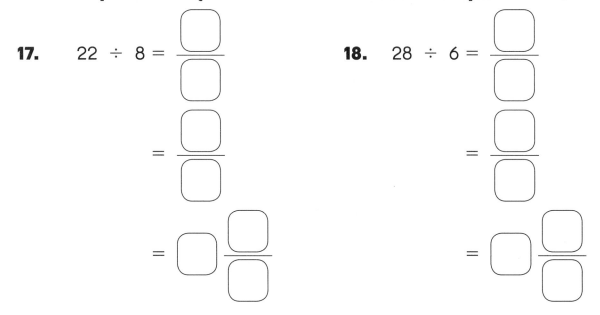

17. 22 ÷ 8 =

18. 28 ÷ 6 =

Express each fraction as a decimal. *(Lesson 3.4)*

19. $\frac{4}{5}$ = _____

= _____

20. $\frac{17}{20}$ = _____

= _____

Express each division expression as a mixed number and as a decimal.
(Lessons 3.3 and 3.4)

	Division expression	Express division expression as	
		a mixed number	a decimal
21.	13 ÷ 4		
22.	23 ÷ 5		

Add. Express each sum in simplest form. *(Lesson 3.5)*

23. $2\frac{2}{7} + 3\frac{1}{2}$

24. $1\frac{1}{2} + 1\frac{5}{9}$

Estimate each sum by using the nearest whole number or half. *(Lesson 3.5)*

25. $1\frac{5}{8} + 1\frac{1}{5}$

26. $2\frac{1}{6} + 3\frac{4}{5}$

Subtract. Express each difference in simplest form. *(Lesson 3.6)*

27. $5\frac{8}{9} - 3\frac{5}{6}$

28. $4\frac{2}{7} - 2\frac{7}{8}$

Estimate difference by using the nearest whole number or half. *(Lesson 3.6)*

29. $2\frac{1}{10} - 1\frac{4}{7}$

30. $3\frac{3}{8} - 1\frac{7}{12}$

Find the product in simplest form. *(Lesson 4.1)*

31. $\dfrac{6}{7} \times \dfrac{5}{8} =$

32. $\dfrac{4}{5} \times \dfrac{10}{12} =$

33. $\dfrac{2}{5}$ of $\dfrac{10}{11} =$

34. $\dfrac{8}{9}$ of $\dfrac{5}{12} =$

Multiply. Express the product in simplest form. *(Lesson 4.3)*

35. $\dfrac{2}{5} \times \dfrac{15}{7} =$

36. $\dfrac{9}{5} \times \dfrac{5}{12} =$

Multiply. Express the product as a whole number or a mixed number in simplest form. *(Lesson 4.3)*

37. $\dfrac{4}{3} \times \dfrac{7}{6} =$

38. $\dfrac{8}{3} \times \dfrac{9}{12} =$

39. $\dfrac{7}{8} \times \dfrac{6}{5} =$

40. $\dfrac{25}{4} \times \dfrac{10}{8} =$

Multiply. Express the product as a whole number or a mixed number in simplest form. *(Lesson 4.4)*

41. $2\dfrac{1}{4} \times 16 =$

42. $27 \times 1\dfrac{2}{9} =$

Multiply. Express the product as a whole number or a mixed number in simplest form. (*Lesson 4.4*)

43. $5\dfrac{3}{6} \times 42 =$ **44.** $2\dfrac{5}{6} \times 15 =$

Divide. Express each quotient in simplest form. (*Lesson 4.6*)

45. $\dfrac{7}{8} \div 5 =$ **46.** $\dfrac{5}{8} \div 4 =$

47. $\dfrac{4}{7} \div 12 =$ **48.** $\dfrac{2}{9} \div 6 =$

Name: _____   Date: _____

Problem Solving

Solve. Show your work.

49. Ron used $\frac{3}{5}$ pound of flour to bake bread and $\frac{2}{7}$ pound of flour to bake scones. How many more pounds of flour did he use to bake bread than scones?

50. Tina uses $4\frac{5}{12}$ yards of wire for her science project. Kelvin uses $1\frac{2}{3}$ yards of wire for his project. How many yards of wire do they use altogether?

51. Rosa poured $1\frac{3}{4}$ quarts of orange juice into a container. She added $3\frac{1}{3}$ quarts of apple juice. She then poured $2\frac{2}{3}$ quarts of the mixed juice into a pitcher.

How many quarts of mixed juice were left in the container?

52. In a marathon, Hamish had to run a total distance of $\frac{11}{12}$ mile. He ran $\frac{4}{5}$ of the distance. How many miles did he run?

53.   Ashley uses $\frac{1}{4}$ of a packet of raisins for a fruit cake. She then uses $\frac{1}{9}$ of the remainder for some biscuits. What fraction of the packet of raisins does she have left?

54.   Mrs. Vernon used $4\frac{3}{8}$ pounds of meat to make one pot of soup. She made 12 equal-sized pots of soup. How many pounds of meat did she use altogether?

55. A custodian pours $\frac{3}{8}$ gallon of cleaning solution equally into 9 pails. Find the volume of solution in two of these pails.

56. A carnival sold 135 bottles of juice in one day. They sold $\frac{1}{3}$ of the bottles in the first hour and $\frac{2}{5}$ of the bottles in the second hour. How many bottles of juice did they sell altogether in these two hours?

57. Ms. Li spent $840 on a vacation. She spent $\frac{2}{3}$ of the amount on a train ticket and $\frac{1}{2}$ of the remaining amount on food. How much did she spend on the ticket and food altogether?

58. Sam traveled $\frac{3}{4}$ of a journey by bus. He jogged $\frac{1}{2}$ of the remaining distance and walked the rest of the way. If he walked 800 feet, what was the total distance he traveled?

59. Matthew used $\frac{1}{5}$ of a box of flour for cooking and $\frac{3}{4}$ of the remainder to make bread. The rest of the flour was packed equally into 5 containers. What fraction of the total amount of flour was in each container?

60. A bus driver filled up $\frac{7}{8}$ of her fuel tank for a trip. She used $\frac{6}{7}$ of the fuel by the end of the trip. The capacity of her tank is 70 gallons. How much fuel did she use for the trip? Express your answer as a decimal.

Chapter

Algebra

Practice 1   Using Letters as Numbers

Write an expression for each situation.

1.   Susan has 10 apples and 6 oranges. How many fruits does she have?

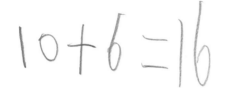

$$10 + 6 = 16$$

2.   Juan has *x* apples and 8 oranges. How many fruits does he have?
     Give your answer in terms of *x*.

$$x + 8$$

3.   Henry has $18. He spends $2. How much does he have left?

$$18 - 2 = 16$$

4.   Katie has *m* dollars. She spends $5. How much does she have left?
     Give your answer in terms of *m*.

$$m - 5$$

Write an expression for the situation.

5. Hugo has $20. He spends *n* dollars. How much does he have left? Give your answer in terms of *n*.

$$20 - n$$

Write an algebraic expression for each of the following.

> **Example**
>
> Add 9 to *y*.
>
> *y* + 9 or 9 + *y*

6. Add *b* to 11.

$$11 + b$$

7. Subtract 6 from *c*.

$$c - 6$$

8. Subtract *p* from 15.

$$15 - p$$

9. 12 more than *d*.

$$d + 12$$

10. 15 less than *g*.

$$9 - 15$$

Evaluate each expression for the given values of *y*.

	Expression	Value of the Expression	
		y = 25	*y* = 16
Example	*y* + 5	30	21
11.	*y* − 12	13	4
12.	18 + *y*	43	34
13.	35 − *y*	50	19

25
−12
‾‾‾
13

35
−16
‾‾‾

18
+16
‾‾‾
34

Write each of the following in at least three other ways.

> **Example**
>
> 6n $6 \times n$, $n \times 6$, 6 groups of n

14. $18 \times m$ _____

_____

15.   75 groups of y _____

_____

16. y groups of 12 _____

_____

Write an expression for each situation.

17.   Julio has 4 boxes of pencils. There are 12 pencils in each box. How many pencils does Julio have?

18.   Tara has k boxes of pencils. There are 10 pencils in each box. How many pencils does Tara have? Give your answer in terms of k.

Write an expression for each situation.

19. A restaurant divided 20 gallons of lemonade among 4 tanks. How much lemonade does each tank contain?

20. m gallons of lemonade is distributed equally among 3 people. How much lemonade does each person get? Give your answer in terms of m.

Write an expression for each situation.

> *Example*
>
> Multiply 4 and g.
>
> $4 \times g = 4g$ or $g \times 4 = 4g$

21. Multiply f and 6.

22. Divide m by 3.

23. Divide 22 by p.

Evaluate each expression for $t = 156$.

> *Example*
>
> $2t = 2 \times t$
> $\quad = 2 \times 156$
> $\quad = 312$

24. $\dfrac{t}{6} =$

25. $16t =$

26. $\dfrac{t}{13} =$

Write an algebraic expression for each situation.

27. A tank has x gallons of water. Ted adds 3 gallons of water into the tank. He pours the water equally into 4 smaller containers. How much water is in each container?

28. Jenny has 15 dollars. She buys 2 books that cost $\$m$ each. How much does she have left?

Write an algebraic expression for each situation.

29.   Betty collected 400 food packages for charity. She gave
_g_ packages to an orphanage, and distributed the rest equally among
4 charities. How many packages did each charity get?

30.   To bake muffins, Matt needs _x_ eggs for every 200 grams of flour.
If he used 900 grams of flour, how many eggs did he use?

Write an expression for each situation.

Example

Subtract 12 from the product of 8 and a.

$8 \times a - 12 = 8a - 12$

31. Add 14 to the product of 3 and b.

32. Divide the product of 7 and d by 5.

Evaluate each expression for $x = 5$.

Example

$$13x - 4 = 13 \times 5 - 4$$
$$= 65 - 4$$
$$= 61$$

33. $5x + 12 =$

34. $20 - 2x =$

35. $\frac{x}{10} + 2 =$

36. $\frac{6x}{5} + 12 =$

Fill in the boxes with the correct expressions. In the last box on the right, evaluate each expression for $m = 28$.

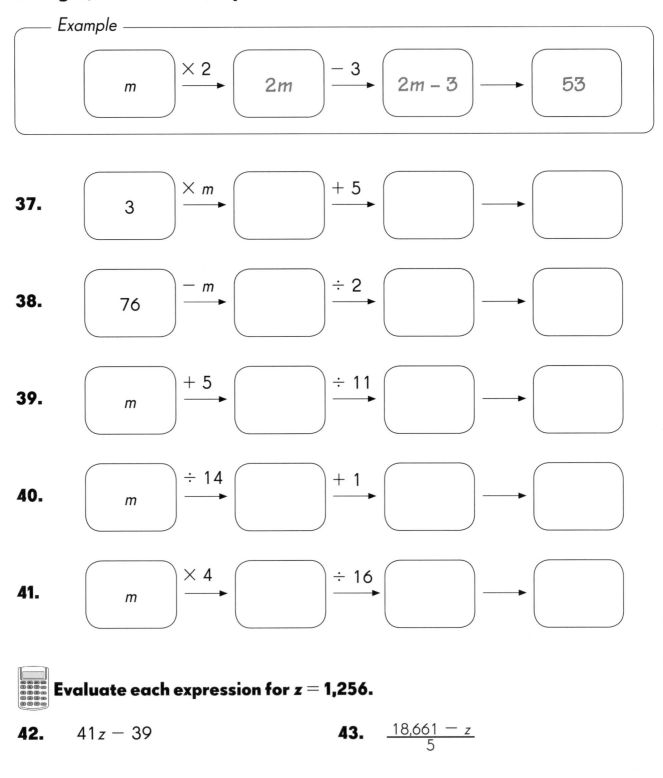

Example

| m | $\times 2$ | $2m$ | $- 3$ | $2m - 3$ | | 53 |

37. 3 $\times m$ ☐ $+ 5$ ☐ → ☐

38. 76 $- m$ ☐ $\div 2$ ☐ → ☐

39. m $+ 5$ ☐ $\div 11$ ☐ → ☐

40. m $\div 14$ ☐ $+ 1$ ☐ → ☐

41. m $\times 4$ ☐ $\div 16$ ☐ → ☐

Evaluate each expression for $z = 1{,}256$.

42. $41z - 39$

43. $\dfrac{18{,}661 - z}{5}$

44. $\dfrac{13z}{8} + 7{,}389$

45. $\dfrac{9z - 1{,}476}{42}$

Practice 2   Simplifying Algebraic Expressions

Simplify each expression.

> *Example*
>
> $c + c + c + c = 4c$

1. $6p + 3p =$

2. $b + 3b + 5b =$

3. $10k - 3k =$

4. $12p - 12p =$

5. $6p - 2p - 3p =$

6. $10a - a + 2a =$

7. $4c + c - 5c =$

8. $10f - 4f + f =$

Simplify each expression.

> *Example*
>
> $5x + 2x + 4 = 7x + 4$

9. $x + 5x - 9 =$

10. $2m + 4 + 6m =$

11. $10p - 4p - 5 =$

12. $4 + 5k - 4k =$

13. $2 + 6b - 1 + 4b =$

14. $5c + 3 - 2c + 5 =$

15. $9e - 2e + 3 + 5e =$

16. $6h + 12 + 2h - 6 =$

Write an algebraic expression for each situation.

17. The length of a piece of fabric is 8y yards. Landon cuts 7 yards from it to make some cushion covers. He then cuts another 3y yards to make a curtain. The remaining material is cut into 4 equal pieces. How long is each piece?

18. Ling has 4m pounds of flour. She buys another 2 packages of flour, each weighing m pounds. How much flour does Ling have now in terms of m?

Write an algebraic expression for each situation.

19.   On Monday, Linus made 5*k* paper cranes and gave 2*k* paper cranes to his friends. On Tuesday, he made another 4*k* paper cranes. His friend gave him 5 paper cranes. How many paper cranes does he have now in terms of *k*?

20.   At the market, a pear costs *b* cents and an apple costs 7 cents less than a pear. Randy buys 4 pears and an apple. How much does Randy pay in terms of *b*?

Practice 3   Inequalities and Equations

Complete with $>$, $<$, or $=$.

1.   For $y = 3$, $6y \bigcirc 11$.

2.   For $y = 6$, $6y \bigcirc 36$.

3.   For $y = 4$, $6y \bigcirc 26$.

4.   For $y = 5$, $6y \bigcirc 24$.

Complete with $>$, $<$, or $=$ for $x = 8$.

5. $3x \bigcirc 20$

6. $5x + 5 \bigcirc 45$

7. $2x - 9 \bigcirc x - 1$

8. $12 - x \bigcirc x \div 2$

Solve each equation.

Example

$$x - 5 = 5$$

$$x - 5 + 5 = 5 + 5$$

$$x = 10$$

$$x = \underline{\quad 10 \quad}$$

9. $2a + 4 = 10$

$a = \underline{\hspace{2cm}}$

10. $5b - 13 = 17$

11. $2m - 3 = m$

$b = \underline{\hspace{2cm}}$

$m = \underline{\hspace{2cm}}$

12. $12n + 7 = 8n + 15$

13. $2s + 16 = 4s - 6$

$n = \underline{\hspace{2cm}}$

$s = \underline{\hspace{2cm}}$

Practice 4 Real-World Problems: Algebra

Solve. Show your work.

1. Raul has 5 boxes of golf balls. Each box contains y golf balls.
    His father gives him another 8 golf balls.

    a. Find the total number of golf balls Raul has in terms of y.

    b. If y = 4, how many golf balls does Raul have altogether?

2. Glenda bought z containers of laundry detergent at $9 each.
    She gave the cashier $50.

    a. Find the change Glenda received in terms of z.

    b. If z = 3, how much change did Glenda receive?

Solve. Show your work.

3.   Garrett is w years old. His mother is 4 times his age.
His father is 3 years older than his mother.

    a.   How old is Garrett's father in terms of w?

    b.   If $w = 9$, how old is Garrett's father?

4.   An office manager bought 16 boxes of pens, each containing
m pens. Workers took 10 pens from the supply room.

    a.   How many pens were left? Give your answer in terms of m.

    b.   If $m = 5$, how many pens were left in the supply room?

Solve. Show your work.

5.   Sarah has a box containing x ribbons and 4 extra ribbons.
Jill has 12 ribbons.

    a.   Express the number of ribbons that Sarah has in terms of x.

    b.   For what value of x will Sarah and Jill have the same number of ribbons?

6.   Henry made $(2y + 4)$ paper cranes. Elise made $(3y - 9)$ paper cranes.

    a.   If $y = 6$, who would have made more paper cranes?

    b.   For what value of y will they have made the same number of
paper cranes?

Solve. Show your work.

7. Mary has *y* yards of fabric. She used 2 yards to sew a skirt. She used the remaining fabric to make 5 jackets.

    a. Find the amount of material that was used to make each jacket in terms of *y*.

    b. If she has 17 yards of fabric, how much material was used for each jacket?

8. A magazine costs half as much as a book. The book costs *p* dollars. A pen costs $2 more than the magazine.

    a. How much does the pen cost in terms of *p*?

    b. If the book costs $5, how much does the pen cost?

Math Journal

John's solutions to the following problems are as shown. Identify and explain the mistakes John has made. Then give the correct solution.

1. $4w + 12w - 10 = 16w - 10$
                              $= 6w$

2. $20p - 2p + 4p = 20p - 6p$
                                $= 14p$

3. $6 \div q = \dfrac{q}{6}$

4. Clarissa bought 3 cartons of milk for y cents each. She gave the cashier $10. How much change did she receive? Express your answer in terms of y.

$3 \times y = 3y$

3 cartons of milk cost $3y$ cents.

$10 - 3y$

Clarrisa received $(10 - 3y)$ dollars as change.

Put On Your Thinking Cap!

Challenging Practice

Wendy bought 7 bags. Each bag costs the same amount. She paid the cashier $100 and received g dollars as change.

a. What was the cost of each bag in terms of g?

b. If the price of each bag was more than $10, what is the least possible value of g? (Assume that the cost of each bag is a whole number.)

Problem Solving

There are 40 pupils in a class. There are x more girls than boys.

a. How many boys are there in terms of x?

b. If $x = 4$, how many boys are there?

Chapter

6 Area of a Triangle

Practice 1 Base and Height of a Triangle

Complete to give both the base and the height in each triangle.

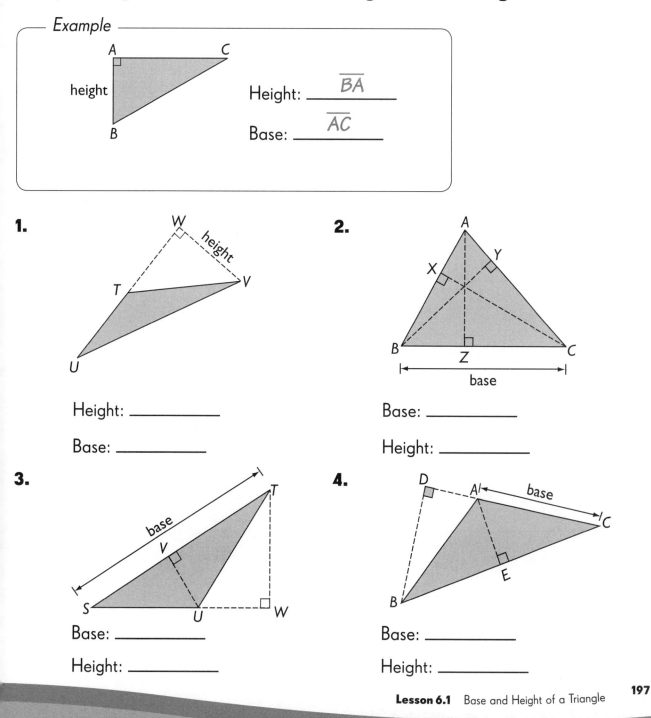

Example

Height: $\overline{BA}$

Base: $\overline{AC}$

1.

Height: _____

Base: _____

2.

Base: _____

Height: _____

3.

Base: _____

Height: _____

4.

Base: _____

Height: _____

For each triangle, the base is given.
Use a drawing triangle to draw the height.
Label the height.

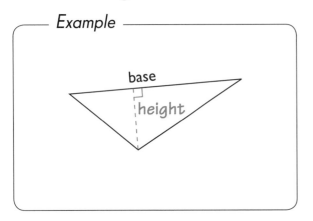

Example

base
height

5.

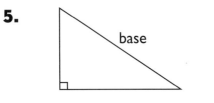

base

6.

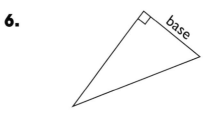

base

7.

base

8.

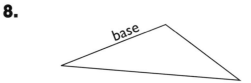

base

9.

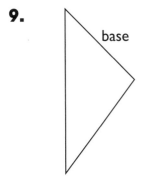

base

10.

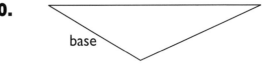

base

Practice 2   Finding the Area of a Triangle

Find the area of each shaded triangle. Show each step and give your answer using the correct units.

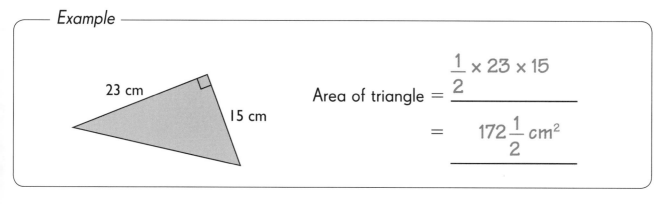

Example

23 cm

15 cm

Area of triangle = $\dfrac{\frac{1}{2} \times 23 \times 15}{\rule{4cm}{0.4pt}}$

$= \dfrac{172\frac{1}{2} \text{ cm}^2}{\rule{4cm}{0.4pt}}$

1.

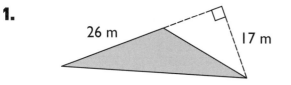

26 m

17 m

2.

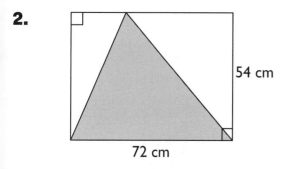

54 cm

72 cm

3.

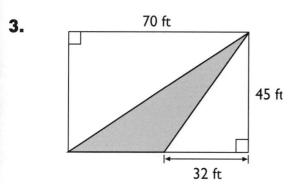

70 ft

45 ft

32 ft

Find the area of each shaded triangle.

Example

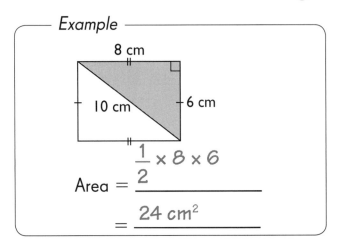

$$Area = \frac{\frac{1}{2} \times 8 \times 6}{}$$

$$= \underline{24 \text{ cm}^2}$$

4.

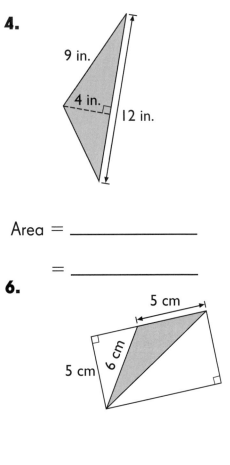

Area = _____

= _____

5.

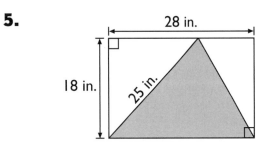

Area = _____

= _____

6.

Area = _____

=

_____

7.

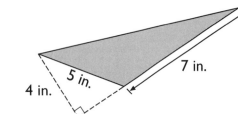

Area = _____

= _____

8.

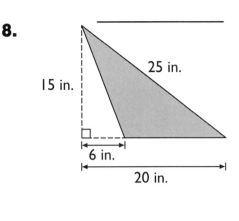

Area = _____

= _____

Math Journal

1.   Four students found the area of the shaded triangle.

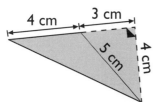

4 cm   3 cm

5 cm   4 cm

These are their findings.

> Zach: $4 \times 4 = 16 \text{ cm}^2$
>
> Preeti: $\frac{1}{2} \times 5 \times 4 = 10 \text{ cm}^2$
>
> Brian: $\frac{1}{2} \times 7 \times 4 = 14 \text{ cm}^2$
>
> James: $\frac{1}{2} \times 3 \times 4 = 6 \text{ cm}^2$

Explain the mistakes they have made. Then write the correct answer.

Zach: _____

Preeti: _____

Brian: _____

James: _____

The area of the shaded triangle is: _____

2.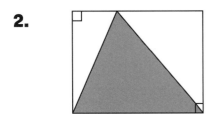

The area of the shaded triangle is 15 cm².
Explain why the area of the rectangle is 30 cm².

3. *ABCD* is a rectangle and *BE = EC*.

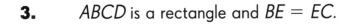
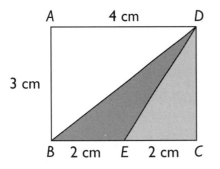

A   4 cm   D

3 cm

B   2 cm   E   2 cm   C

What can you say about the areas of triangles *BED* and *ECD*?

Explain your answer.

Put On Your Thinking Cap!

Challenging Practice

Solve. Show your work.

1. *ABCD* is a square of side 10 cm and *BE* = *EC*.
Find the area of the shaded triangle.

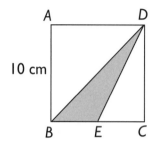

2. *ABCD* is a rectangle 18 cm by 8 cm.
AE = *ED* and *AF* = *FB*. Find the area
of the shaded triangle.

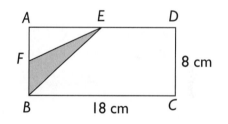

3. *ABCD* is a rectangle of area 48 square inches. The length of *CD* is 3 times the length of *DF*. *BC* = 4 in.

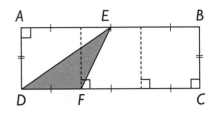

a. Find the length of *DF*.

b. Find the area of the shaded triangle.

4. *ABCD* is a rectangle 12 cm by 5 cm. *BE* = 4 cm. Find the area of the shaded region, *ABED*.

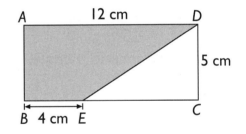

5.   The side of square *ABCD* is 8 cm. *AE* = *AF* = 4 cm.
Find the area of the shaded triangle, *CEF*.

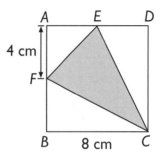

6.   The perimeter of rectangle *ABCD* is 256 inches. Its length is 3
times as long as its width. Find the area of triangle *ABC*.

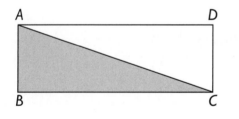

7. ABCD is a rectangle of area 72 square centimeters.
The length of AD is 3 times the length of AE.
BF = 8 cm.

a. Find the width of the rectangle.

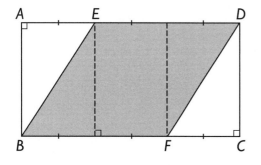

b. Find the area of the shaded region, EBFD.

Put On Your Thinking Cap!

Problem Solving

1. Look at the pattern of these triangles.

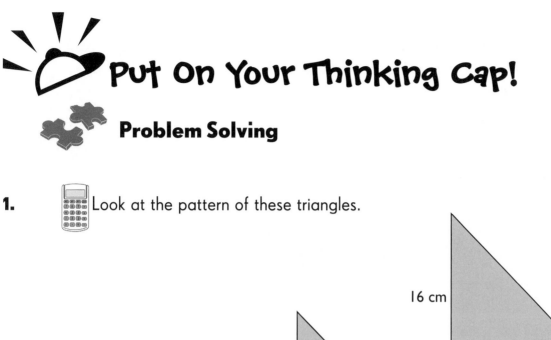

Triangle 1	Triangle 2	Triangle 3	Triangle 4

2 cm, 2 cm — Triangle 1
4 cm, 4 cm — Triangle 2
8 cm, 8 cm — Triangle 3
16 cm, 16 cm — Triangle 4

What is the area of Triangle 5 in the pattern? _____

Which triangle in the pattern will have an area of 32,768 cm²? _____

2. *ABCD* is a square with sides of 20 cm. *AX* = *XB*, *BY* = *YC*, *CZ* = *ZD*, *AW* = *WD*. *WY* and *XZ* are straight lines. Find the total area of the shaded parts.

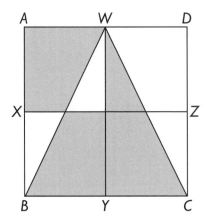

Ratio

Practice 1   Finding Ratio

The table shows the number of points each student scored in a math game.

Find the total number of points the students scored.

1.

Student	Number of Points
Yolanda	8
Sue	3
Norita	5
Vanna	11
Total	

Complete the table to show the ratios.

2.

The ratio of ...	Ratio
the number of points Yolanda has to the number of points Vanna has is	8 : 11
the number of points Norita has to the number of points Sue has is	
the number of points Sue has to the number of points Norita has is	
the number of points Yolanda has to the total number of points is	
the total number of points to the number of points Vanna has is	

Complete.

Mr. Gonzales put some pencils into bundles of 10. He gave 4 bundles to Charlie and 9 bundles to Lisa.

3. The ratio of the number of pencils Charlie has to the number of pencils Lisa has is _____ : _____.

4. The ratio of the number of pencils Lisa has to the number of pencils Charlie has is _____ : _____.

5. The ratio of the number of pencils Lisa has to the total number of pencils is _____ : _____.

This table shows the amount of milk and spring water that four families drink in a week.

Find the total amount of milk and water that they drink.

6.

Family	Amount of Milk	Amount of Spring Water
Lee	4 qt	6 gal
Modano	9 qt	9 gal
Santos	13 qt	10 gal
Willis	5 qt	7 gal
Total		

Use the above table to fill in the blanks.

Example

The ratio of the amount of water the Santos family drinks to the amount of water the Modano family drinks is ____10 : 9____.

7. The ratio of the amount of milk the Modano family drinks to the amount of milk the Willis family drinks is _____.

Name: _____ **Date:** _____

Use the table on page 210 to fill in the blanks.

8. The ratio of the amount of water the Willis family drinks

to the amount of water the Lee family drinks is _____.

9. The ratio of the total amount of milk to the amount of milk the

Modano family drinks is _____.

10. The ratio of the amount of water the Santos family drinks to the

total amount of water is _____.

When writing two quantities as a ratio, the quantities must be in the same unit. The ratio itself however has no units.

Complete.

11. The ratio of the length of A to the length

of C is _____ : _____.

12. The ratio of the length of C to the length

of B is _____ : _____.

13. The ratio of the length of A to the total length

of A, B, and C is _____ : _____.

Complete.

14. The ratio of the length of R to the length

of P is _____ : _____.

15. The ratio of the length of P to the length

of Q is _____ : _____.

16. The ratio of the length of P to the total length

of P, Q, and R is _____ : _____.

Draw models to show each ratio.

17.   5 : 9

18.   12 : 7

Solve.

19.   Grandma gave $15 to Linda and Dianne. Linda got $7.

   a.   How much money did Dianne get?

   b.   Find the ratio of the amount of money Linda got to the amount of money Dianne got from Grandma.

Solve.

20. Amelia has 25 postcards. She gives 8 away.

    a. How many postcards does she have left?

    b. Find the ratio of the number of postcards Amelia has left to the number of postcards she had at first.

21. Clark has two 16-ounce cans of corn. He uses 18 ounces of it to make a corn soup and the rest to make a casserole.

    a. How many ounces of corn did he use to make the casserole?

    b. What is the ratio of the amount of corn Clark used to make the casserole to the amount of corn he had at first?

22. In a supermarket bin, the number of packages of red peppers to the number of packages of green peppers is in the ratio 8 : 13. The peppers are sold in 2-pound packages.

a. What is the least possible weight of red peppers in the bin?

b. What is the least possible weight of green peppers in the bin?

Leanne put 6 counters into a bag. She took out some counters from the bag but not all of them.

Find the ratio of the number of counters taken out from the bag to the number of the counters left in the bag. Make a list of all possible ratios using the table.

23.

Number of Counters Taken Out	Number of Counters Left in the Bag	Ratio
1	5	1 : 5

Practice 2   Equivalent Ratios

Write ratios to compare the two sets of items.

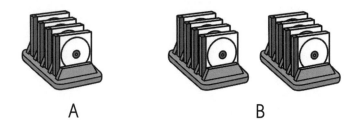

A   B

1.   The ratio of the number of CDs in Group A to the number of CDs in

Group B is _____ : _____.

2.   The ratio of the number of CD-holders in Group A to the number of

CD-holders in Group B is _____ : _____.

3.   _____ : _____ = _____ : _____ in simplest form.

Write ratios to compare the two sets of items.

A   B

4.   The ratio of the number of pencils in Group A to the number of pencils in

Group B is _____ : _____.

5.   The ratio of the number of bundles in Group A to the number of bundles in

Group B is _____ : _____.

6. $18 : 27 = 6 : 9 =$ _____ : _____ in simplest form.

Find the greatest common factor of each set of numbers.

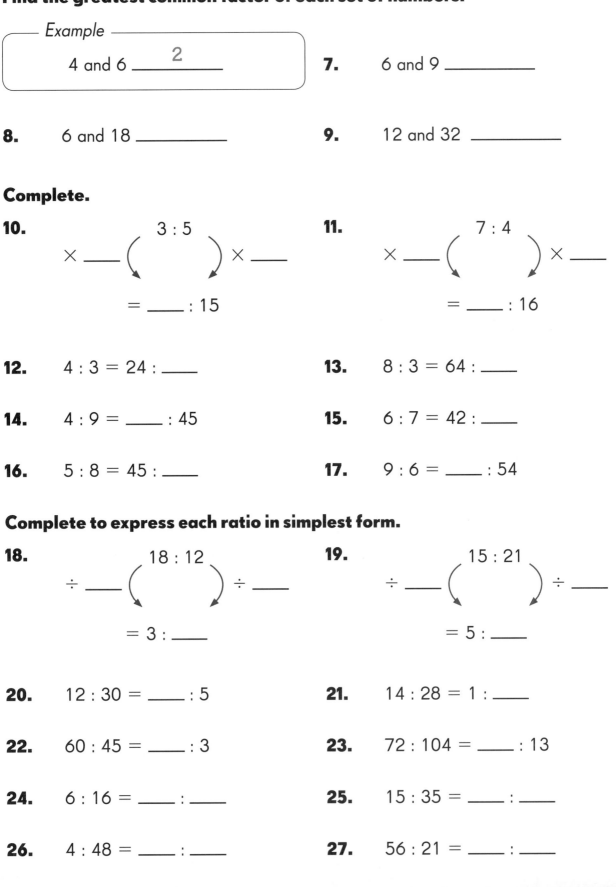

Example

4 and 6 ___2___

7. 6 and 9 _____

8. 6 and 18 _____

9. 12 and 32 _____

Complete.

10.

$$\times \underline{\quad} \overset{3 : 5}{\huge(\qquad)} \times \underline{\quad}$$

$$= \underline{\quad} : 15$$

11.

$$\times \underline{\quad} \overset{7 : 4}{\huge(\qquad)} \times \underline{\quad}$$

$$= \underline{\quad} : 16$$

12. $4 : 3 = 24 : \underline{\quad}$

13. $8 : 3 = 64 : \underline{\quad}$

14. $4 : 9 = \underline{\quad} : 45$

15. $6 : 7 = 42 : \underline{\quad}$

16. $5 : 8 = 45 : \underline{\quad}$

17. $9 : 6 = \underline{\quad} : 54$

Complete to express each ratio in simplest form.

18.

$$\div \underline{\quad} \overset{18 : 12}{\huge(\qquad)} \div \underline{\quad}$$

$$= 3 : \underline{\quad}$$

19.

$$\div \underline{\quad} \overset{15 : 21}{\huge(\qquad)} \div \underline{\quad}$$

$$= 5 : \underline{\quad}$$

20. $12 : 30 = \underline{\quad} : 5$

21. $14 : 28 = 1 : \underline{\quad}$

22. $60 : 45 = \underline{\quad} : 3$

23. $72 : 104 = \underline{\quad} : 13$

24. $6 : 16 = \underline{\quad} : \underline{\quad}$

25. $15 : 35 = \underline{\quad} : \underline{\quad}$

26. $4 : 48 = \underline{\quad} : \underline{\quad}$

27. $56 : 21 = \underline{\quad} : \underline{\quad}$

Practice 3 Real-World Problems: Ratios

Solve. Show your work.

1. Ms. Grande bought 24 apples and 18 oranges for a party after
    a class play. Find the ratio of the number of apples to the total
    number of fruits Ms. Grande bought.

2. There are 44 chicken and fish filets altogether in a freezer. There are
    12 chicken filets. What is the ratio of the number of chicken filets
    to the number of fish filets in the freezer?

Solve. Show your work.

3.   There were 12 boys and 18 girls in a class. Then, 3 more boys joined the class and 2 girls left. What is the ratio of the number of boys to the number of girls in the class now?

4.   Monica had $42 and Naomi had $18 at first. Monica then gave $6 to Naomi. What is the ratio of the amount of money Monica has to the amount of money Naomi has in the end?

Solve. Show your work.

5.   In a competition, the ratio of the number of tickets Mark collected to the
number of tickets Julia collected is 4 : 3. Julia collected 36 tickets.
How many tickets did they collect altogether?

6.   The ratio of the number of stamps Calvin has to the number of stamps
Roger has is 7 : 3. Roger has 18 stamps. How many stamps do they
have altogether?

Solve. Show your work.

7. On a Saturday, the ratio of the amount of water used by Household A to the amount of water used by Household B was 13 : 5. Household A used 260 gallons of water for that day. Find the total amount of water used by the two households on that Saturday.

8. A cleaning solution and water are mixed in the ratio 4 : 15. The amount of water in the mixture is 1,200 milliliters. What is the total volume of the mixture?

Practice 4   Ratio in Fraction Form

Write your answer in the box.

1.   Which model correctly shows that 'A is $\frac{7}{4}$ times B'?

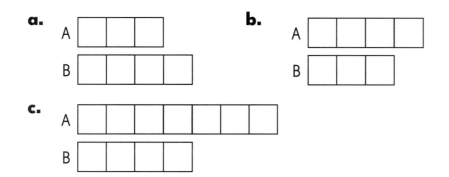

a. A, B   **b.** A, B   **c.** A, B   ☐

Complete.

The ratio of the lengths of Stick A and Stick B are as shown.

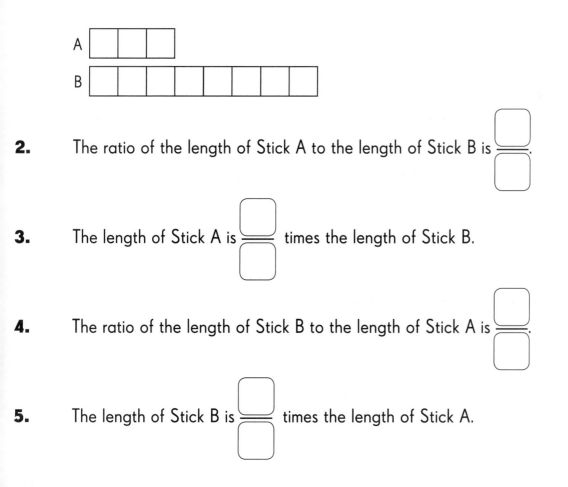

2.   The ratio of the length of Stick A to the length of Stick B is $\dfrac{\square}{\square}$.

3.   The length of Stick A is $\dfrac{\square}{\square}$ times the length of Stick B.

4.   The ratio of the length of Stick B to the length of Stick A is $\dfrac{\square}{\square}$.

5.   The length of Stick B is $\dfrac{\square}{\square}$ times the length of Stick A.

Complete.

The diagram shows the masses of two bags of rice, X and Y.

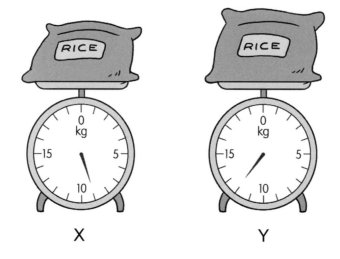

X   Y

6. The mass of Y is $\dfrac{\boxed{}}{\boxed{}}$ times the mass of X.

7. The mass of X is $\dfrac{\boxed{}}{\boxed{}}$ times the mass of Y.

8. The ratio of the mass of X to the total mass of X and Y

is _____ : _____.

9. The mass of X is $\dfrac{\boxed{}}{\boxed{}}$ times the total mass of X and Y.

10. The mass of Y is $\dfrac{\boxed{}}{\boxed{}}$ times the total mass of X and Y.

Solve.

11.   Pete played 18 tennis matches in a week. Jack played 6 fewer matches than Pete.

       a.   How many tennis matches did Jack play in that week?

       b.   Find the ratio of the number of matches Pete played to the total number of matches both boys played. Give your answer in fraction form.

       c.   How many times the number of matches Pete played is the number of matches Jack played?

Solve. Draw a model to help you.

12. Kenny's weight is $\frac{6}{7}$ times Melvin's weight.

    a. What is the ratio of Kenny's weight to Melvin's weight? Give your answer in fraction form.

    b. What is the ratio of Melvin's weight to the total weight of the two boys? Give your answer in fraction form.

    c. How many times the total weight of the two boys is Kenny's weight?

Solve.

13. Kimberly is 3 times as old as her sister, Halley.

    a. Find the ratio of Kimberly's age to Halley's age. Give your answer in fraction form.

    b. Find the ratio of Halley's age to their total age. Give your answer in fraction form.

    c. How many times Kimberly's age is Halley's age?

    d. How many times their total age is Kimberly's age?

Solve.

14. In a college library, there are 4 times as many nonfiction books as fiction books.

    a. Find the ratio of the number of nonfiction books to the number of fiction books. Give your answer in fraction form.

    b. How many times the number of nonfiction books is the number of fiction books?

    c. Suppose the number of fiction books is $\frac{2}{7}$ times the number of nonfiction books. What would be the ratio of the number of nonfiction books to the total number of books? Give your answer in fraction form.

Practice 5   Comparing Three Quantities

Find the greatest common factor for each set of numbers.

	Set of Numbers	Greatest Common Factor
Example	2, 6 and 8	2
1.	5, 10 and 20	
2.	3, 9 and 15	
3.	6, 24 and 27	

Complete to express each ratio in simplest form.

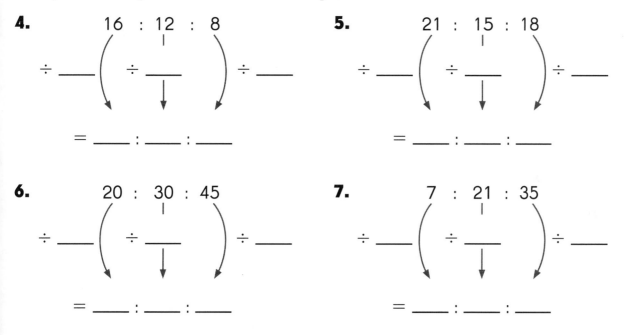

4.   16 : 12 : 8

÷ ___ (÷ ___) ÷ ___

= ___ : ___ : ___

5.   21 : 15 : 18

÷ ___ (÷ ___) ÷ ___

= ___ : ___ : ___

6.   20 : 30 : 45

÷ ___ (÷ ___) ÷ ___

= ___ : ___ : ___

7.   7 : 21 : 35

÷ ___ (÷ ___) ÷ ___

= ___ : ___ : ___

Express each ratio in simplest form.

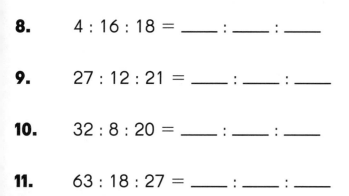

8.   4 : 16 : 18 = ___ : ___ : ___

9.   27 : 12 : 21 = ___ : ___ : ___

10.   32 : 8 : 20 = ___ : ___ : ___

11.   63 : 18 : 27 = ___ : ___ : ___

Complete.

12.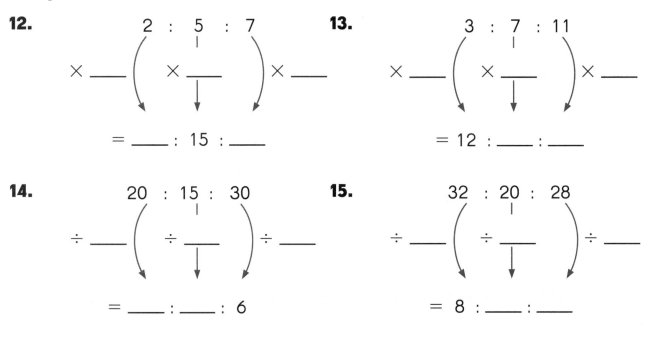

$$2 : 5 : 7$$
$$\times \underline{} \left(\times \frac{}{} \right) \times \underline{}$$
$$= \underline{} : 15 : \underline{}$$

13.

$$3 : 7 : 11$$
$$\times \underline{} \left(\times \frac{}{} \right) \times \underline{}$$
$$= 12 : \underline{} : \underline{}$$

14.

$$20 : 15 : 30$$
$$\div \underline{} \left(\div \frac{}{} \right) \div \underline{}$$
$$= \underline{} : \underline{} : 6$$

15.

$$32 : 20 : 28$$
$$\div \underline{} \left(\div \frac{}{} \right) \div \underline{}$$
$$= 8 : \underline{} : \underline{}$$

Complete.

16. $1 : 2 : 5 = \underline{} : 6 : \underline{}$

17. $7 : 4 : 3 = 28 : \underline{} : \underline{}$

18. $4 : 5 : 9 = \underline{} : 25 : \underline{}$

19. $16 : 14 : 6 = \underline{} : \underline{} : 3$

20. $18 : 24 : 30 = \underline{} : 4 : \underline{}$

21. $35 : 42 : 56 = 5 : \underline{} : \underline{}$

Practice 6   Real-World Problems: More Ratios

Solve. Show your work.

1.   For a school fair, Lolita's parents donated 4 bottles of orange juice,
10 bottles of fruit punch and 8 bottles of apple juice.
Find the ratio of the number of bottles of orange juice to the number
of bottles of fruit punch to the number of bottles of apple juice
Lolita's parents donated.

2.   A company gave a total of $900 to three charities. Charity A
received $200, Charity B received $400 and Charity C received
the remaining amount. What is the ratio of the amount Charity A received
to the amount Charity B received to the amount Charity C received?

Solve. Show your work.

3. Ruth cuts a piece of string into three parts. Their lengths are in the ratio 2 : 3 : 5. The longest part is 35 centimeters long. How long is the shortest part?

4. The ages of three brothers, Dave, Randy, and Martin, are in the ratio 1 : 2 : 3. Dave is 7 years old. Find the total age of all three brothers.

Solve. Show your work.

5.   The number of dolls that Lisa, Mia, and Nina have are in the ratio 6 : 4 : 7.
Nina has 21 dolls.

    a.   How many dolls does Lisa have?

    b.   What is the total number of dolls that the three girls have?

6.   Amin, Barb, and Curt collected seashells in the ratio of 10 : 12 : 7. Curt
collected 98 seashells. How many seashells did they collect together?

Solve. Show your work.

7. By the end of a year, Kieran's savings is $\frac{9}{2}$ of Simon's savings.

    a. What is the ratio of Kieran's savings to Simon's savings to their total savings?

    b. How many times the total amount of money saved is Kieran's savings?

    c. How many times the total amount of money saved is Simon's savings?

    d. Simon saves $28 less than Kieran. How much do both of them save altogether?

Solve. Show your work.

8. Lita, Kala, and Rose entered a typing competition. Lita typed 2 times
    as fast as Kala. The ratio of the number of words Kala typed to
    the number of words Rose typed was 4 : 1. If Rose typed 48 words,
    how many words did Lita type?

Solve. Show your work.

9.   Camry's Dairy Factory produces milk in three flavors: vanilla, strawberry, and chocolate. The amount of vanilla-flavored milk they produce in a day is 2 times the amount of chocolate-flavored milk. The amount of chocolate-flavored milk they produce in a day is 3 times the amount of strawberry-flavored milk.

   a.   What is the ratio of the amount of vanilla-flavored milk to the amount of chocolate-flavored milk to the amount of strawbery-flavored milk it produces in a day?

   b.   How many times the total amount of milk produced is the amount of vanilla-flavored milk produced?

Math Journal

Andy and Clara each drew a model to solve this word problem.

Mr. Marcos bought chicken and beef from the butcher and fish from the fish market for a barbecue. The ratio of the weight of chicken to the weight of beef to the weight of fish he bought was 3 : 1 : 5. He bought 10 pounds of fish. What was the total weight of meat he bought from the butcher?

Both models however are incorrect.
Explain the mistakes that they each made.

Andy's model

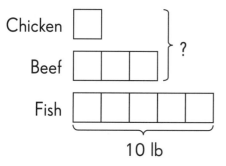

Andy's model is incorrect because

_____

_____

_____

_____

Clara's model

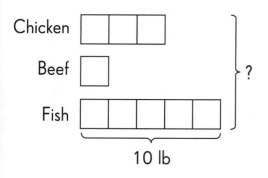

Clara's model is incorrect because

_____

_____

_____

_____

Draw the correct model. Then solve the problem.

Put On Your Thinking Cap!

Challenging Practice

1. A small square of area 16 square centimeters is cut from a larger square with sides that measure 6 centimeters. Find the ratio of the area of the small square to the area of the remaining part of the larger square.

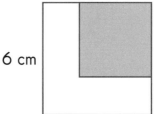

6 cm

2. The perimeters of two squares are in the ratio 2 : 4. The perimeter of the larger square is 16 centimeters.

a. What is the perimeter of the smaller square?

b. What is the length of one side of the smaller square?

Put On Your Thinking Cap!

Problem Solving

Solve.

1. The ratio of the number of plants Trish bought to the number of plants Sarah bought is 2 : 5. Trish bought 16 plants.

  a. What is the total number of plants Trish and Sarah bought altogether?

  b. If each plant cost $17, what is the total cost of the plants Trish and Sarah bought?

2. The ratio of the number of boys to the number of girls at a town fair is 5 : 8. There are 60 boys at the fair.

  a. What is the total number of boys and girls at the fair?

  b. The admission fee for each child is $3. Find the total admission fees for the boys and girls.

for Chapters 5 to 7

Concepts and Skills

Evaluate each expression for $x = 5$. *(Lesson 5.1)*

1. $x + 9$

2. $16 - x$

3. $4x$

4. $\dfrac{x}{5}$

Simplify each expression. *(Lesson 5.2)*

5. $y + 3y$

6. $a + a - 2$

7. $3b + 5b - 2b$

8. $8c + 6 - 1 - c$

Complete with =, >, or < for _d_ = 7. *(Lesson 5.3)*

9. $d + 7 \bigcirc 15$

10. $3d - 10 \bigcirc 11$

11. $2d + 6 \bigcirc 3d - 2$

12. $(35 \div d) + 5 \bigcirc d$

Solve each equation. *(Lesson 5.3)*

13. $2e = 8$

14. $3f + 3 = 18$

$e =$ _____

$f =$ _____

15. $6g - 5 = 2g + 3$

16. $4h - 11 = h + 16$

$g =$ _____

$h =$ _____

Complete to give both the base and the height in each triangle. *(Lesson 6.1)*

17.

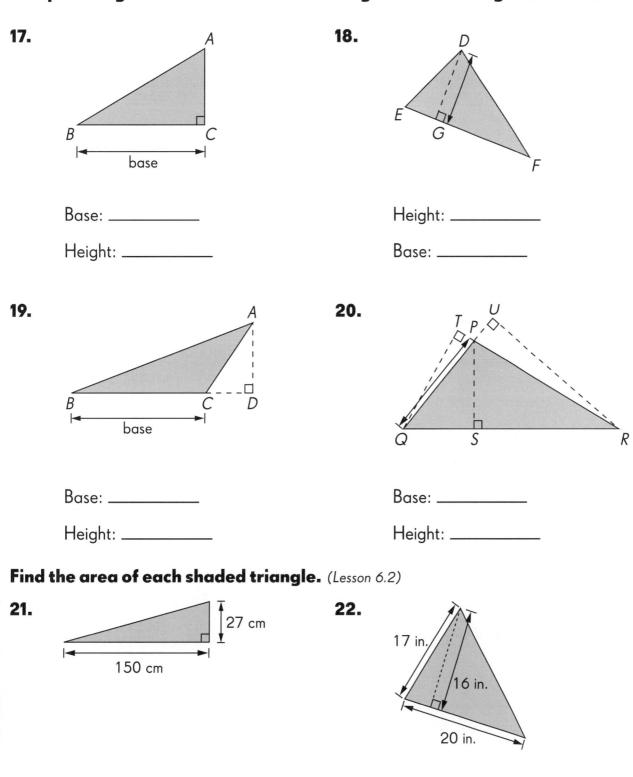

Base: _____

Height: _____

18.

Height: _____

Base: _____

19.

Base: _____

Height: _____

20.

Base: _____

Height: _____

Find the area of each shaded triangle. *(Lesson 6.2)*

21.

27 cm

150 cm

22.

17 in.

16 in.

20 in.

Area = _____

Area = _____

Find the area of each shaded trtiangle. *(Lesson 6.2)*

23.

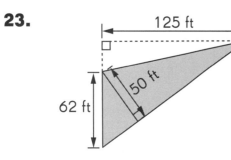

Area = _____

24.

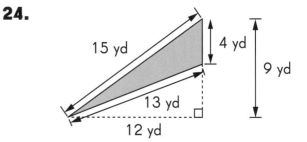

Area = _____

25.

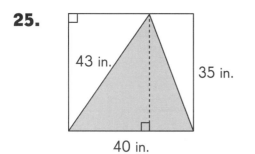

Area = _____

26.

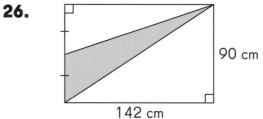

Area = _____

Find the total area of the shaded parts. *(Lesson 6.2)*

27.

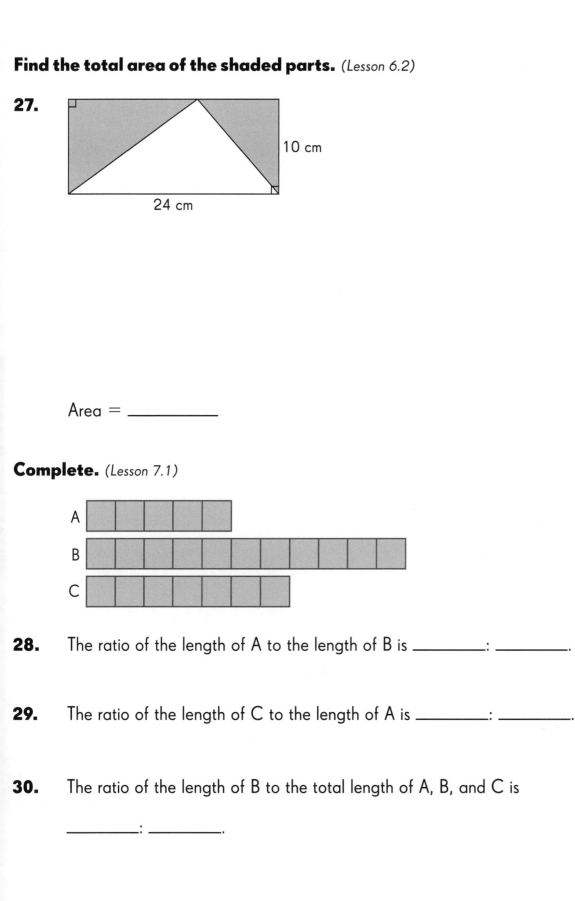

10 cm

24 cm

Area = _____

Complete. *(Lesson 7.1)*

A

B

C

28.   The ratio of the length of A to the length of B is _____ : _____.

29.   The ratio of the length of C to the length of A is _____ : _____.

30.   The ratio of the length of B to the total length of A, B, and C is

_____ : _____.

Complete. *(Lesson 7.2)*

Set A	Set B

31. The ratio of the number of squares in Set A to the number of squares in

Set B is _____ : _____.

32. The ratio of the number of groups in Set A to the number of groups in

Set B is _____ : _____.

33. _____ : _____ = _____ : _____ in simplest form.

Find the missing number or term in each set of equivalent ratios. *(Lesson 7.2)*

34. $7 : 4 = 21 :$ _____

35. $5 : 9 =$ _____ $: 63$

36. $18 : 21 = 6 :$ _____

37. $108 : 72 =$ _____ $: 6$

Name: _____ **Date:** _____

Complete. *(Lesson 7.4)*

The heights of two buildings are shown.

38. The ratio of the height of Math Plaza to the height of

Focus Tower is $\dfrac{\boxed{}}{\boxed{}}$.

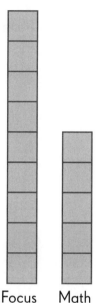

39. The height of Math Plaza is _____ times

the height of Focus Tower.

40. The height of Focus Tower is _____ times

the height of both buildings.

Focus Tower   Math Plaza

Express each ratio in simplest form. *(Lesson 7.5)*

41. $8:12:24 =$ ____ : ____ : ____ **42.** $21:9:36 =$ ____ : ____ : ____

Find the missing numbers or terms in each set of equivalent ratios. *(Lesson 7.5)*

43. $4:6:9 = 24:$ ____ : ____ **44.** $48:56:28 =$ ____ : ____ : 7

Problem Solving

Solve. Show your work.

45. Mandy scores b points in a basketball game. Jay scores 3 points less than Mandy. Kareem scores 2 times as many points as Mandy.

    a. Find the number of points that Jay scores in terms of b.

    b. Find the total number of points the three players score in terms of b.

46. David reads a book that has $(3x + 6)$ pages. Ellen reads a book that has $(4x - 4)$ pages.

    a. If $x = 7$, whose book has more pages?

    b. For what value of x will the two books have the same number of pages?

Solve. Show your work.

47. In the figure, $BC = 18$ cm and $AD = CD$. The length of CD is twice the length of BC. Find the area of the shaded triangle ABC.

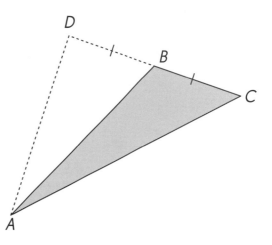

48. $ABCD$ is a rectangle with a width of 12 centimeters. Its length is twice as long as its width. $AE = 12$ centimeters and $AF = BF$. Find the area of the shaded triangle CEF.

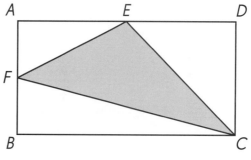

Solve. Show your work.
Give your answer in either ratio form or fraction form.

49. There were 45 pennies in Container A and 79 pennies in Container B at first. Suki took 7 pennies out from Container A. She then put them into Container B.

    a. What is the ratio of the number of pennies in Container A to that in Container B at first?

    b. Find the ratio of the number of pennies in Container A to that in Container B in the end. Express your answer in simplest form.

Solve. Draw a model to help you.

50. Peggy cycles 3 times as far as Dakota.
    a. Find the ratio of the distance that Peggy cycles to the distance
         that Dakota cycles. Give your answer in fraction form.

    b. How many times the combined distance is the distance that Peggy cycles?

Solve. Show your work.

51.   A company makes yearly donations to Charities A, B, and C in the ratio
            3 : 7 : 9. It donates $5,096 to Charity B in a year.
    a.   How much does it donate to Charity A in a year?

    b.   How much does it donate to all three charities in a year?

52.   The ratio of the number of boys to the number of girls in a camp is 3 : 7.
            There are 24 boys in the camp.
    a.   How many girls are there in the camp?

    b.   The camp fee is $50 per person. Find the total amount of fees
            the girls pay.

Mid-Year Review

Test Prep

Multiple Choice

Fill in the circle next to the correct answer.

1. Which of the following is 3,450,026 in word form? *(Lesson 1.1)*

   (A) Three million, four hundred fifty thousand, twenty-six

   (B) Three million, four hundred thousand fifty, twenty-six

   (C) Three million, fifty thousand four hundred, twenty-six

   (D) Three million, forty-five thousand, twenty-six

2. Which number is the greatest? *(Lesson 1.3)*

   (A) 15,265   (B) 93,216

   (C) 320,182   (D) 320,128

3. Which number when rounded to the nearest thousand is 23,000? *(Lesson 1.4)*

   (A) 22,097   (B) 22,499

   (C) 23,400   (D) 23,501

4. Simplify $20 + 10 \times 19 - 7$. *(Lesson 2.6)*

   (A) 140   (B) 203

   (C) 360   (D) 563

5. Which is 1,000 less than the product of 3,021 and 79? *(Lesson 2.3)*

   (A)   2,100   (B)   4,100

   (C)   237,659   (D)   239,659

6. Which is the difference between the value of the digit 6 in 2,300,628 and in 846,150? *(Lesson 1.2)*

   (A)   600   (B)   5,400

   (C)   5,522   (D)   6,000

7. Which is the remainder when 4,885 is divided by 21? *(Lesson 2.5)*

   (A)   12   (B)   13

   (C)   14   (D)   15

8. Express $\frac{8}{11} \div 4$ in simplest form. *(Lesson 4.6)*

   (A) $\frac{2}{11}$ (B) $\frac{8}{44}$

   (C) $\frac{1}{11}$ (D) $\frac{4}{11}$

9. Find the difference: $\frac{3}{4} - \frac{3}{8}$. *(Lesson 3.2)*

   (A) $\frac{5}{8}$ (B) $\frac{3}{8}$

   (C) $\frac{1}{2}$ (D) $\frac{1}{4}$

10. Find the product: $\frac{3}{4} \times \frac{8}{12}$. *(Lesson 4.1)*

   (A) $\frac{1}{2}$ (B) $\frac{2}{3}$

   (C) $\frac{5}{12}$ (D) $\frac{11}{16}$

11. Estimate the sum of $\frac{6}{7}$ and $\frac{3}{5}$. *(Lesson 3.1)*

(A) 0

(B) $\frac{1}{2}$

(C) $1\frac{1}{2}$

(D) 1

12. What is the difference between $3\frac{1}{2}$ and $1\frac{1}{4}$? *(Lesson 3.6)*

(A) $2\frac{1}{4}$

(B) $3\frac{1}{4}$

(C) $4\frac{3}{4}$

(D) $4\frac{1}{2}$

13. Find the area of triangle *ABC*. *(Lesson 6.2)*

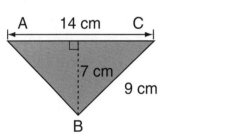

(A) 126 cm²

(B) 98 cm²

(C) 63 cm²

(D) 49 cm²

14. Simplify $4x + 6 - 2x - 1$. *(Lesson 5.2)*

(A) $6x + 7$

(B) $4x + 3$

(C) $8x + 6$

(D) $2x + 5$

15. For what value of y will the inequality $3y + 4 < 8$ be true? *(Lesson 5.3)*

(A) $y = 1$

(B) $y = 2$

(C) $y = 3$

(D) $y = 4$

16. Glass A contains 236 milliliters of milk. Glass B contains 420 milliliters of milk. What is the ratio of the amount of milk in Glass A to that in Glass B? *(Lesson 7.3)*

(A) 89 : 135

(B) 119 : 165

(C) 479 : 660

(D) 59 : 105

Short Answer

Read the questions carefully. Write your answers in the space provided. Show your work.

17. What is the missing number in the box? *(Lesson 1.2)*

$$87,412 = 80,000 + \boxed{} + 400 + 10 + 2$$

_____

18. Order the numbers from greatest to least. *(Lesson 1.3)*

35,928   164,239   35,982   916,236

_____

19. Rounding to the nearest thousand, what is the least number that rounds to 32,000? *(Lesson 1.4)*

_____

20. Find the product of 238 and 4,000. *(Lesson 2.2)*

_____

21. There are 215 Grade 5 students in Cherrywood school. Each student spends $17 on a dictionary. How much in all do the students spend on the dictionary? *(Lesson 2.7)*

_____

22. Mr. Hull is buying computer equipment for his company. The equipment costs $45,900. He pays $5,300 for the first payment. He then pays the rest of the amount in equal payments for 14 months. Find the amount he has to pay each month. *(Lesson 2.7)*

_____

23. Simplify $(2 + 4) \times 7 - 6 + 11$. *(Lesson 2.6)*

_____

24. Express $38 \div 6$ as a fraction in simplest from. Then rewrite the fraction as a mixed number. *(Lesson 3.3)*

_____

25. Shaun has $24\frac{1}{2}$ ounces of beads. He has $3\frac{3}{8}$ ounces of beads less than Tony. Find the weight of Tony's beads. *(Lesson 3.7)*

_____

26. Express $24\frac{1}{4} - 15\frac{1}{2}$ as a decimal. *(Lessons 3.3 and 3.6)*

_____

27. Lita jogged $7\frac{3}{10}$ kilometers on Friday. She jogged $1\frac{3}{4}$ kilometers more on Saturday. How many kilometers did she jog on both days? Give your answer as a decimal. *(Lesson 3.7)*

_____

28. Multiply $\frac{70}{6}$ by $\frac{18}{4}$. Express the product as a mixed number in simplest form. *(Lesson 4.3)*

_____

29. Jamal runs $1\frac{2}{5}$ miles a day to train for a race.

    a. If he runs the same distance for 3 days a week, what is the distance he runs in one week?

    b. If he keeps to this training regime for 8 weeks, what is the total distance he will run in 8 weeks ? *(Lesson 4.5)*

a. _____

b. _____

30. A ball of string $\frac{9}{10}$ meter long is cut into 3 pieces of the same length.

Find the length of each piece. *(Lesson 4.6)*

_____

31. 3 batteries cost $5r and 8 folders cost $2r. Jason bought
6 batteries and 4 folders. How much does he pay?
Give your answer in terms of r. *(Lesson 5.4)*

_____

32. Solve this equation. *(Lesson 5.3)*
$4a - 8 = a + 4$

_____

33. The base of the triangle *ABC* is as given.
Label its height . *(Lesson 6.1)*

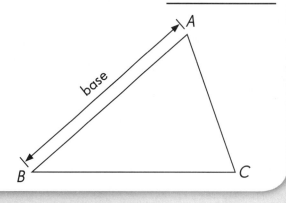

34. Find the area of triangle *PQR*. *(Lesson 6.2)*

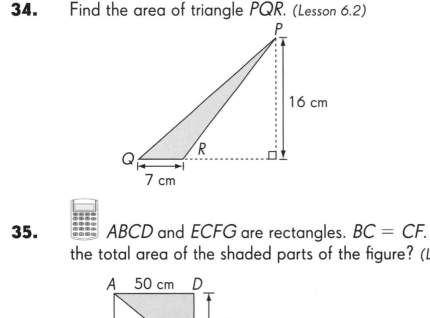

35. ABCD and ECFG are rectangles. BC = CF. What is the total area of the shaded parts of the figure? *(Lesson 6.2)*

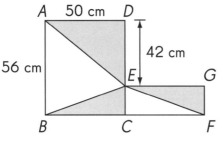

36. The ratio of the masses of flour in two bags is 5 : 7. The heavier bag contains 1,120 grams of flour. What is the total mass of flour in both bags? *(Lesson 7.3)*

37. Rachel, Sally, and Fabio share a pie in the ratio 1 : 2 : 4. What fraction of the pie does Sally get? *(Lesson 7.6)*

38. 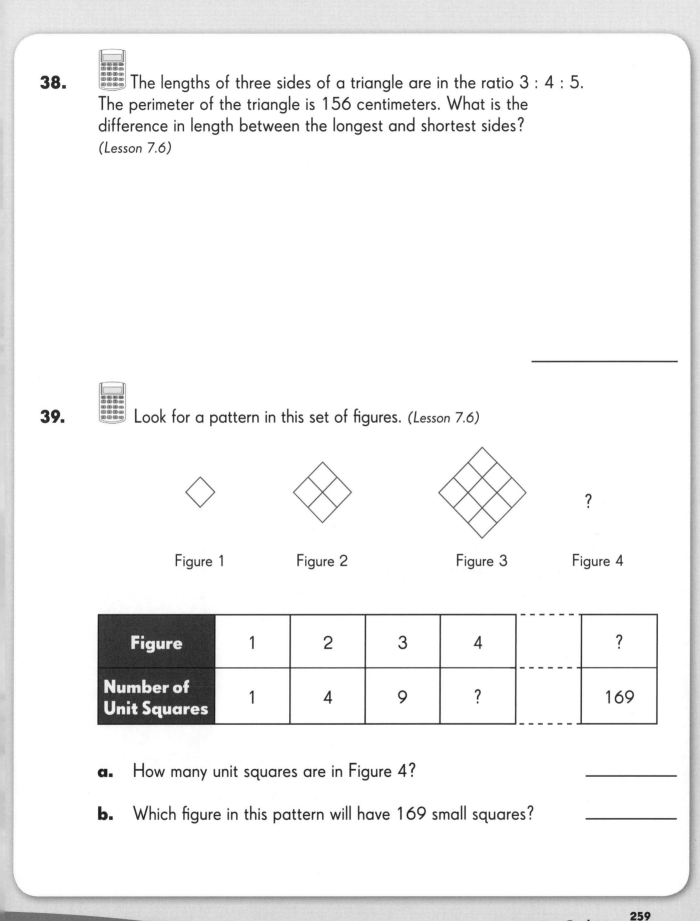 The lengths of three sides of a triangle are in the ratio 3 : 4 : 5. The perimeter of the triangle is 156 centimeters. What is the difference in length between the longest and shortest sides?
(Lesson 7.6)

_____

39. Look for a pattern in this set of figures. *(Lesson 7.6)*

| Figure 1 | Figure 2 | Figure 3 | Figure 4 |

Figure	1	2	3	4		?
Number of Unit Squares	1	4	9	?		169

a. How many unit squares are in Figure 4?   _____

b. Which figure in this pattern will have 169 small squares?   _____

Extended Response

Solve. Show your work.

40. Poles are placed an equal distance apart along a 6-kilometer road. There is a tree in between every two poles. The figure shows the distance between a tree and two poles. Poles are placed at the start and end of the road. How many poles are there? *(Lesson 2.4)*

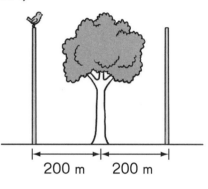

200 m   200 m

41. A whole number when divided by 4 gives a remainder of 3. The same whole number when divided by 6 gives a remainder of 1. The number is between 70 and 85. What is the number? *(Lesson 2.5)*

42. Sarah earns $525 more than Andrew each month. They each spend $1,250 a month and save the rest. Sarah does not have any savings at first. After 11 months, she has $8,250 in savings. How much does Andrew earn in a year? *(Lesson 2.7)*

43. Ivan caught a total of $7\frac{2}{5}$ pounds of fish one day. Of the fish caught, $4\frac{5}{8}$ pounds were sea bass and the rest were mackerel. He gave away $1\frac{7}{8}$ pounds of mackerel. How many pounds of mackerel did he have left? Give your answer as a decimal. *(Lesson 3.7)*

44. There were $2\frac{4}{5}$ quarts of milk in Container A and some milk in Container B.

Lisa poured $1\frac{2}{5}$ quarts of milk each into Container A and Container B.

In the end, the total volume of milk in the two containers was 10 quarts.

How many quarts of milk were in Container B at first? Give your answer as a decimal. *(Lesson 3.7)*

45. Tyrone read a book for his school project. On the first day, he read 40 pages. On the second day, he read $\frac{1}{4}$ of the remaining pages.

After the second day, he still had to read $\frac{1}{2}$ of the total number of pages to complete the book. How many pages are in the book? *(Lesson 4.2)*

46.   A dealership has 9y cars, 12y trucks and 18 vans. *(Lesson 5.4)*

  a.   4y cars, 3y trucks and 15 vans are sold. Find the total number of vehicles remaining in terms of y.

  b.   If the value of y is 7, are there more trucks or more cars and vans at first?

47.   The side of square JKLM is 14 inches. KP = MP = JP = LP. Find the total area of the shaded parts. *(Lesson 6.2)*

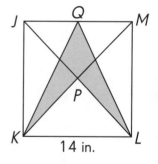

48. Freddie has 2 times as many comic books as David. The ratio of the number of comic books David has to the number of comic books Gary has is 5 : 3. Freddie has 110 comic books. How many comic books do David and Gary have in total? *(Lesson 7.6)*

49. The ratio of the volume of water in Container A to the volume of water in Container B to the volume of water in Container C is 2 : 3 : 8. Container B contains 900 milliliters of water. *(Lesson 7.6)*

a. What is the volume of water in Container C?

b. Find the total volume of water in the three containers.